Quick and Easy
Indian Vegetarian

BY

Veena Chopra

foulsham
LONDON · NEW YORK · TORONTO · SYDNEY

foulsham

The Publishing House, Bennetts Close,
Cippenham, Berkshire, SL1 5AP, England.

Dedication

I dedicate this book to:

Late Mrs Jaswant Kaur Ahluwalia - my beloved mother

Late Mrs Vidhyawati Chopra - my beloved mother-in-law

Mr Bal Krishan Ahluwalia - my father

Pritam Das Chopra - my husband

Sumeet Chopra - my son

Sajni Chopra - my daughter

ISBN 0-572-01886-X

Printed in Great Britain by
Cox & Wyman Ltd, Reading, Berkshire.

CONTENTS

ABOUT THE AUTHOR

Veena Chopra was born in the Punjab and grew up in a large household with many relatives and several servants living together . Educated in Uttar Pradesh, she was an enthusiastic cook from childhood. In 1959 she received 1st prize for cooking in the Shajhanpur district. Veena was trained as a teacher and is a graduate of Agra University, India.

In 1970, Veena was married to a man whom she had met only once for half an hour, a few days before the wedding. The marriage was arranged, as was traditional, by her parents. Veena and her husband, a physics teacher, left for England four days after the marriage. They now live in Cambridge and have two children called Sumeet and Sajni.

In addition to working as science co-ordinator at Blue Gate Fields Junior School, Veena also teaches evening classes in Indian cookery at many Community Colleges in Cambridge-shire. She has given six hour cookery demonstrations on a number of occasions and is a popular speaker at various Women's Institute centres.

Veena is also an accomplished dancer, and with her two children she has given demonstrations of traditional Indian dances at local cultural exhibitions and at various venues in London. She also enjoys playing the sitar. This is Veena's third book and she is working on her fourth.

INTRODUCTION

I have prepared this book for all of you who enjoy Indian cooking, but have little time to spend on its preparation. Many of the dishes in this book can be prepared in less than 15 minutes. An extensive ingredients list is not essential and I have taken care to use only the minimum of spices and still retain the authentic flavour.

I believe that it is important to eat healthily. I remember my mother used to praise the medicinal properties of the many spices used in Indian cooking: ginger is good for digestion; garlic looks after the blood pressure; garam masala protects you from colds and coughs; cloves can relieve toothache; turmeric cleans the blood and sonf and tymol seeds aid digestion and prevent stomach ache. I am sure that you will also benefit.

It was my son and daughter, who are both studying at university, who first gave me the inspiration for this book. They made me realise that students have neither the time nor the money to spare on cooking, but, if given an opportunity still enjoy eating interesting food. So it was with them, and with all of us who have insufficient time in our busy lives and need to be conscious of our weekly budgets, in mind that I wrote this book.

Convenience foods have only been included in the ingredients lists when they have been thoroughly tested and compare favourably with the original.

I would like to thank my family and friends for helping to

test many of the recipes, all of them were used to traditional Indian cookery and their enthusiasm for my quick recipes greatly encouraged me.

All the recipes in this book were designed to serve 2 people, unless stated otherwise. The quantities allow for generous helpings provided you are eating a complete meal i.e. starter, bread, lentil, vegetable and yoghurt dish. You may wish to double the ingredients when cooking for more people, when doing this you should always be careful to add the liquid ingedients gradually and beware of using too many spices.

I hope that you will all enjoy cooking and eating the many different dishes and that you will be encouraged to serve these quick and easy recipes to your families and guests. Remember that your food will taste excellent if prepared cheerfully.

Hints & Tips

Always remember to read the recipe through completely at least once before actually starting to cook. Do not be put off by the large number of ingredients; most of these are standard spices which any Indian cook keeps in their cupboard and once you start cooking Indian food you will use them again and again. The following are a few handy hints to help with your cooking.

1. THE BASIC SPICES you will need in order to cook any dish in this book are: mustard and cumin seeds, coriander (cilantro), ground red chilli, ground turmeric, garam masala (see the recipe on page 13) and green cardamom. Keep them in separate jars and they will keep their aroma for months.

2. BREAD: Frying bread
(a) When deep frying bread do not roll it in dry flour as it burns and this will discolour the cooking fat.
(b) When rolling a chapati or paratha do not use too much dry flour because it burns quickly and gives a dark, burnt look to the bread.
(c) Do not throw bread into the middle of the hot frying pan. The hot oil may splash and this can be dangerous. Slip a puri or bhutoora, katchori, breadroll, samosa, etc., in gently from the edge of the frying pan.

3. BURNT DISHES: If you have burnt your dish, do not scrape from the bottom of the pan. Place the top of the dish in a clean saucepan and carry on cooking.

4. CAULIFLOWER: A white coloured cauliflower is always fresher, more tender and sweeter than a yellow one.
To grate a whole cauliflower, take a knife and start slicing about 2mm thick along the top. Grate the stems using a grater as this will save you time.

5. COOKING TIME: All the cooking times are approximate because a lot depends on the quantity and quality (tenderness and age) of the food you want to cook. Preparation times will vary depending on the skill and experience of the cook. It is possible to save time by preparing the next set of ingredients while the first part of the recipe is cooking.

6. CUMIN: (a) When added to hot oil, cumin takes only 2 seconds to brown.
(b) To roast, place a dry flat frying pan over a medium heat, add the cumin seeds. Stir until golden brown. Turn off the heat, but keep on stirring. Leave to cool. Coarsely grind and keep in an airtight jar.

7. DOUGH: In the recipes you will find dough described as soft, hard or stiff. In each case I have given the quantity of water necessary, but at times you will have to adjust slightly the quantity depending on the texture and moisture of the flour.

8. FROZEN FOOD: Most of the cooked Indian food can be frozen, unless stated otherwise (in the recipe).
(a) If frozen foods are used in any of the recipes then naturally the dish should not be re-frozen. If using frozen peas (for example), freeze the food and add the peas when reheating.
(b) If any dish has been frozen, then sufficient time should be allowed for the food to be completely defrosted before reheating.

9. GARAM MASALA: Always sprinkle a little ground garam

masala over a dish before serving so that it retains its pleasant aroma. Whole garam masala (cloves, peppercorns, cinnamon stick and black cardamom) retains its fragrance for a long time, therefore I add it at the beginning.

10. GARLIC AND GINGER: Always peel and wash before chopping or grinding.

11. GREEN CORIANDER AND GREEN CHILLI: Do not be put off trying a recipe because you do not have these fresh spices just miss them out. However it is always nice to buy some when cooking for guests. Try growing fresh coriander in a window box on your windowsill by planting some whole coriander seeds.

12. GRIND: your own spices, except turmeric which is too hard for an electric grinder and red chilli because it will make you sneeze. Home ground spices are cheap and keep their fragrance for a very long time. Do not mix the spices, except to make garam masala, as different spices keep their aromas for different periods of time.

13. HOTNESS OF FOOD: It is difficult to say how hot a dish is because it depends on an individual taste. Red and green chilli in a dish make it hot, therefore increase or decrease the quantity of chillies according to your taste. Food will be delicious even with just a pinch of ground red chilli.

14. LEMON: Always add lemon juice at the end, once the lentils and vegetables are cooked and tender, otherwise they will take longer to cook.

15. LENTILS: In India, lentils or dal have quite a runny consistency. Do not overcook lentils or they will become thick and lose their flavour

16. LID: It is better to close the lid on a saucepan while cooking because:
(a) The food cooks quicker.

(b) The food retains its nutritional value.
(c) The fragrance of the spices is not lost.
(d) The food is cooked in the steam.

17. MEASUREMENT: All teaspoons are level.
Onion size: (a) Small   50 g (2 oz)
            (b) Medium 100 g (4 oz)
            (c) Large   200 g (7 oz)
American measurements are less precise than Metric or Imperial, so when making dough, for example, remember to add the liquid gradually.

18. MICROWAVE OVENS: The popularity of the microwave oven is increasing rapidly. It can be used to defrost and it is marvellous for reheating cooked food, especially rice dishes.

19. MILK: Always rinse your saucepan before adding milk to boil. This will prevent milk sticking to the pan.

20. MUSTARD SEEDS: When frying, cover the pan to avoid making the fat spit.

21. OIL: (a) To check that the oil is sufficiently hot slip a little dough or batter or a thin slice of onion into the hot oil, it should sizzle and come up at once.
(b) Left-over fried oil should be kept separate and used only for frying.
(c) Never fry vegetables in the oil in which you have fried fish, meat or chicken.
(d) Always use fresh oil for dishes (e.g. curries).

22. ONION: Always wash onions after peeling. If they make you cry, soak them in cold water for a little while, or peel them under water. After peeling, cut them in half and leave them on one side for 10 minutes before you start chopping.

23. POPPY SEEDS: They are often quite dirty. Soak them in lukewarm water, drain, dry and grind them in a coffee grinder.

24. PRESSURE COOKER: Using a pressure cooker can save time when cooking chickpeas and lentils. If using a pressure cooker, reduce the quantity of water stated in the recipe.

25. RICE: (a) To see if any remaining water is left after cooking rice, tip the pan a little, but do not stir. Place pan back on a high heat and dry off any remaining water. Close the lid and leave for at least 5 minutes before serving.
(b) Stir cooked rice gently with a fork before serving.
(c) Rice is very delicate when cooked, therefore it is best eaten immediately.

26. SALT: During the summer, Indians replace the salt which they lose through perspiration by drinking salty lemon squash and eating savoury yoghurt dishes. Add salt according to taste. Indians tend to use more salt because it enhances the flavour.

27. SAVING TIME: (a) When peeling onions, cut them in half lengthwise, put the flat side face down on the chopping board. Make lots of parallel cuts along the length. Holding the slices together, cut across the onion.
(b) While one dish is cooking, make dough, prepare rice, or chop onions for the next day.

28. SPICES: It is best to grind your own spices, like coriander (cilantro), cumin and garam masala, because:
(a) The spices are cleaned.
(b) They are fresh and whole spices store better.
(c) They are pure and not a mixture of other spices.
(d) They are full of fragrance.

29. TYMOL SEEDS: Tymol seeds contain quite a lot of dirt, therefore you must clean, soak and drain them in a strainer before use.

30. UTENSILS: For cooking, a saucepan or a frying pan should be heavy. When possible, use stainless steel or enamel-ware saucepans because some of the ingredients like tamarind, lemon, mango, cooking apples, etc. contain acid.

31. VEGETABLES, FRESH AND FROZEN: You can use fresh instead of frozen vegetables and vice versa, but always remember that fresh vegetables require slightly longer cooking time than frozen.

32. WHOLE SPICES: I like to add cloves, cinnamon, black pepper and black cardamoms to a curry while frying the onion. Whole spices retain their fragrance for longer periods than garam masala (after grinding the above spices, one makes garam masala). In India, most people extract the whole spices from their meal, if by mistake, you chew them whole they are very strong. If you or your guests are unfamiliar with the spices then please leave the whole spices out of your dish completely and instead add an extra 2.5 ml/½ tsp garam masala to your recipe.

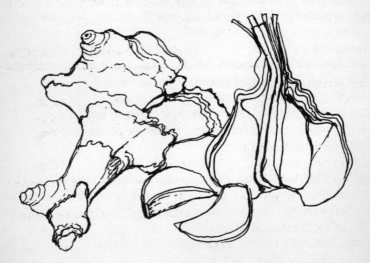

BASIC RECIPES

GARAM MASALA

Make your own garam masala. There is no comparison between home-made garam masala and that bought from a shop. You can keep the home-made garam masala in an airtight container for at least three months without it losing its aroma.

Makes 100 g/4 oz	Metric	Imperial	American
Black cardamoms, use seeds only	*30 ml*	*2 tbsp*	*2 tbsp*
Black peppercorns	*30 ml*	*2 tbsp*	*2 tbsp*
Cloves	*30 ml*	*2 tbsp*	*2 tbsp*
Cinnamon stick, break into small pieces	*30 ml*	*2 tbsp*	*2 tbsp*

1.   Grind the above ingredients in a coffee grinder until they form a powder.

GHEE

Clarified butter

Many families in Northern India prefer to cook in ghee rather than oil. This is actually very fattening, although sweets do taste a lot better if ghee is used.

Makes 450 g/1 lb	Metric	Imperial	American
Butter	*550 g*	*1¼ lb*	*2½ cups*

1. Put the butter in a large saucepan and boil carefully, stirring until all the butter has melted.

2. When the solids (whey) appear at the bottom and the clear part (ghee) is at the top, reduce the heat. Keep on stirring until the liquid becomes light brown. Turn the heat off and continue to stir so that it does not boil over. Allow to cool slightly.

3. Strain the contents of the saucepan through a muslin (cheesecloth) cloth into a container or jar.

4. Squeeze the remaining ghee through the muslin and discard the contents of the cloth. Let the ghee cool down. Place the lid on the container and keep to one side until required.

5. The cloth can be reused after washing. Ghee can be kept for months in an airtight container.

KHOYA
Solidified milk

Khoya is solidified milk. Traditionally people reduce the milk by boiling until it solidifies like dough. It is used mainly in sweet making.

Traditional way of making khoya

Makes 600 ml/1 pt	Metric	Imperial	American
Milk, gold top	1.2 l	2 pt	5 cups

1. Place the milk in a large heavy-bottomed saucepan and bring to the boil. Reduce the heat to medium-low and keep stirring from time to time until the milk solidifies. It will take about 2 hours.

Quick way of making khoya

	Metric	Imperial	American
Full cream milk powder (non-fat dry milk)	50 g	2 oz	½ cup
Ghee, melted	10 ml	2 tsp	2 tsp
Milk, lukewarm	30 ml	2 tbsp	2 tbsp

1. Combine all the above ingredients in a bowl, mix together well. The mixture should have the consistency of a soft dough.

PANEER

Indian Cheese

In India people like to make cheese at home. Indian cheese is quite different in taste from English and Continental cheese. If you fry paneer, it becomes softer and more spongy when cooked.

Makes 150 g/ 5 oz	Metric	Imperial	American
Pasteurised milk	*1.2 l*	*2 pt*	*5 cups*
Lemon juice	*60 ml*	*4 tbsp*	*4 tbsp*

1. Boil the milk. Immediately add the juice to make the milk separate into curds and whey. Leave to set for 5 minutes. Do not throw away the whey because it is rich in minerals and can be used in curries instead of water to give extra flavour.

2. Line a strainer with a muslin cloth (cheesecloth), strain the milk and squeeze out the excess whey. Fold the cloth around the paneer to form a square, about 7½ cm (3 in). Place on an upturned plate and put a heavy weight or a larger saucepan filled with water on top to squeeze out any remaining whey. Leave for at least 4 hours to set.

When used in curries, cut the paneer into small pieces, 1 cm (½ in) square, and fry in a deep frying pan over a medium heat until light golden brown or bake on a greased tray in a pre-heated oven at 200° C/400° F/gas mark 6 for 5 minutes. Do not fry the paneer if it is to be used in a sweet recipe.

UBLÉ ALOO

Potatoes Boiled in Jackets

Potatoes are probably the cheapest vegetable and are used abundantly in Indian cooking. It is quite usual to have unexpected visitors in India and extra potatoes are always boiled in their jackets in the morning in readiness. This means that at breakfast potato paratha can be cooked, puri wale aloo for a main meal, aloo bonda at tea-time can all be prepared on the spur of the moment.

Serves 2	Metric	Imperial	American
Potatoes, washed	*550 g*	*1¼ lb*	*1¼ lb*
Water	*1.2 l*	*2 pts*	*5 cups*

1. Place the potato and the water in a large saucepan. Bring to the boil, reduce the heat, close the lid and cook for 15-20 minutes or until tender.

ROASTED CUMIN

When I say ground cumin in a recipe, it refers to roasted ground cumin.

Makes 50 g/2 oz	Metric	Imperial	American
Cumin, cleaned	*50 g*	*2 oz*	*4 tbsp*

1. Heat a tawa or flat frying pan over a medium-low heat. Place the cumin in it and keep turning over for 2 minutes or until brown. Cool and grind coarsely. Keep in an airtight jar. For best results use within a month of grinding.

TAMARIND PULP

Tamarind trees are large and shady and that is why they are planted on the edges of roads. During the heat of summer people and livestock take shelter under them. We used to pick-up unripened tamarind on our way to school and eat them with salt and pepper. These fruit are very sour and one should not eat too many. The tamarindi are picked when ripe, the stones are removed and after drying they are packed in bars. These bars will keep for at least a year. Tamarinds contain iron and vitamin C.

	Metric	Imperial	American
Dry tamarind, soaked over-night or boiled in 300 ml/ ½ pt/1¼ cups water for 15 minutes on a medium-low heat.	*100 g*	*4 oz*	*8 tbsp*

1. Extract pulp from soaked or boiled and cooked tamarind and throw away the seeds and the sticks etc. (the waste shouldn't exceed 15 ml/1 tbsp). I use 300 ml (½ pt/ 1¼ cups) of cold water to extract the pulp and never add more than 45 ml (3 tbsp) or 60 ml (4 tbsp) water at a time to sieve pulp.

STARTERS & SAVOURY SNACKS

In India, friends and relations may visit at any hour of the day and the host will always offer them something special to eat and drink.

MÃDHI

Mãdhi is a snack and it is made in different sizes for different occasions. For daily consumption, the madhies are made in a small size, but for weddings larger 30 cm (12 in) in diameter madhies, and 1 cm (½ in) thick are made. The edges are pinched to make an attractive pattern.

Makes 12	Metric	Imperial	American
Plain (all-purpose) flour, sifted	100 g	4 oz	½ cup
Margarine	5 ml	1 tsp	1 tsp
Tymol seeds, cleaned	2.5 ml	½ tsp	½ tsp
Black peppercorns, crushed by a rolling pin	6	6	6
Salt	large pinch	large pinch	large pinch
Water, lukewarm	45 ml	3 tbsp	3 tbsp
Oil for deep frying			

1. To make the dough rub the margarine into the flour.

2. Add the tymol seeds, black peppercorns and salt and mix.

3. Gradually add the water to make a dough. Knead the dough for about 1 minute or until the dough is springy and smooth.

4. Cover and leave for 5 minutes.

5. Place the oil in a deep frying pan over a medium heat.

6. While the oil is heating, roll the dough into a sausage shape and cut it into 12 portions.

7.   Shape each piece into a ball in the palm of your hands and then roll out into a thin circle about 7.5 cm (3 in) in diameter.

8.   Take a pointed knife and make 10-12 small slits all over the circle.

9.   Add 6 madhies at a time to the hot oil. Turn them over a few times and fry until light brown on both sides.

10. Remove them with a slotted spoon and set them on a cooling tray to cool. Repeat until you have fried all the madhies.

Serving suggestions

Serve them freshly-made, hot or cold, with pickle or dhaniya chutney or any sweet at tea-time. The madhies can be kept in an airtight container for up to a fortnight.

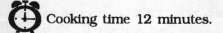 Cooking time 12 minutes.

NAMAKPARÉ

Namakparé is a crispy snack which can be eaten at any time with a drink. Namakparé will keep for a fortnight in an air-tight container. If you want to make double the quantity then do so because it will add only 3 to 4 minutes extra to your frying time.

Serves 2	Metric	Imperial	American
Plain (all-purpose) white flour	75 g	3 oz	³/₄ cup
Lemon juice	10 ml	2 tsp	2 tsp
Tymol seeds (ajwain), cleaned	2.5 ml	¹/₂ tsp	¹/₂ tsp
Salt	1.25 ml	¹/₄ tsp	¹/₄ tsp
Water	45 ml	3 tbsp	3 tbsp
Oil for frying			

1. Place the flour, lemon juice, tymol seeds and salt in a bowl. Gradually add the water to make a soft but not sticky dough. Knead for 1 minute or until the dough is springy and smooth. Cover and leave for 10 minutes.

2. For rolling you will need a handful of plain flour and a little oil.

3. Place the oil in a deep frying pan on medium-low heat.

4. While the oil is heating, shape the dough into a ball in the palm of your hands and then roll out into a thin square.

5. Smear the square with 5 ml (1 tsp) oil and sprinkle over about 5 ml (1 tsp) flour. Bring one edge over (fold in half) to make a rectangle and again smear the surface with the same quantities of oil and flour. Bring an edge over again to give it a square shape. Repeat this once again

to give you a lot of crunchy layers. Roll out the square till it is 5 mm (¼ in) thick.

6. Take a pointed knife and make 1 cm (½ in) parallel lines across the square. Make another set of 1 cm (½ in) parallel lines to cross the first and form a diamond shape. Make sure you cut right through the dough.

7. Add all the namakparé to the hot oil and fry slowly until light brown.

8. Remove from the oil with a slotted spoon and leave to cool.

Serving suggestions

Serve cold at tea-time with gulab jamun or any sweet.

Cooking time 10 minutes.

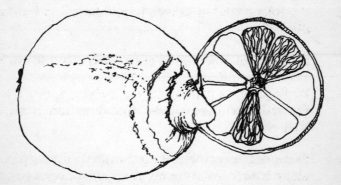

PANEER TIKKA
Cheese Chops

Paneer Tikka is a wonderful starter for a meal or it can be served as a tea-time snack. I also use it to garnish pulao. You will find it to be of medium hotness. Paneer is an Indian word for cheese (see page 16).

Serves 2	Metric	Imperial	American
Paneer (see page 16), cut into 3 mm ($^1/_8$ in) thick and 2.5 cm (1 in) long pieces	100 g	4 oz	$^1/_2$ cup
Lemon juice	10 ml	2 tsp	2 tsp
Sugar	10 ml	2 tsp	2 tsp
Natural (plain) yoghurt	10 ml	2 tsp	2 tsp
Large garlic clove, crushed	1	1	1
Fresh ginger, crushed or grated	1 cm	$^1/_2$ in	$^1/_2$ in
Garam masala	2.5 ml	$^1/_2$ tsp	$^1/_2$ tsp
Tymol seeds, cleaned	2.5 ml	$^1/_2$ tsp	$^1/_2$ tsp
Ground coriander (cilantro)	2.5 ml	$^1/_2$ tsp	$^1/_2$ tsp
Ground red chilli	2.5 ml	$^1/_2$ tsp	$^1/_2$ tsp
Salt, to taste			
Oil	25 ml	$1^1/_2$ tbsp	$1^1/_2$ tbsp

1. Place all the above ingredients, except the oil, in a bowl and rub the mixture onto the paneer pieces.

2. Heat a flat frying pan (tava) over a medium heat. Pour in the oil.

3. Place one paneer piece at a time into the frying pan. Put a little leftover mixture on top of the paneer pieces.

4. Turn them over after 1 minute and put the rest of the mixture on the paneer pieces. Keep turning every so often and fry until lightly golden brown.

Serving suggestions

Serve hot with coriander (cilantro) chutney, and eat with a toothpick.

Cooking time 5 minutes.

DHANIYA WALÉ ALOO
Potatoes in Coriander Chutney

Dhaniya walee aloo is a delicious dish. It can be used as a part of 'chat' or as a side dish to accompany any meal.

Serves 2 - 3	Metric	Imperial	American
Small potatoes 1 cm (¹/2 in), boiled in jackets, peeled and used whole or potatoes, boiled in jackets, peeled and cut into 1 cm (¹/2 in) pieces	*250 g*	*9 oz*	*9 oz*
Dhaniya Chutney (see recipe on page 138)			

1. Mix the small potatoes or chopped potato pieces into the dhaniya chutney.

PÃPRI

The pāpri can be eaten as a snack or as one of the items of 'chat'. It is very crispy and delicious. In India, young girls spend most of their pocket money on chat, chocolate, or sweets. In every school and college, you will find at least one chat stall and a long queue of keen buyers during lunch-time and after school.

Makes 9	Metric	Imperial	American
Plain (all-purpose) flour, sifted	75 g	3 oz	³/₄ cup
Lemon juice	5 ml	1 tsp	1 tsp
Tymol seeds (ajwain)	2.5 ml	¹/₂ tsp	¹/₂ tsp
Salt	large pinch	large pinch	large pinch
Water, lukewarm	45 ml	3 tbsp	3 tbsp
Oil for frying			

1. Place the flour, lemon juice, tymol seeds and salt in a bowl. Gradually pour in the water to make a soft, but not sticky dough. Knead the dough for 1 minute or until it is soft, springy and smooth. Cover and leave for 10 minutes.

2. Divide the dough into 9 equal portions. Take a portion and shape it into a ball in the palm of your hands, flatten it, put a few drops of oil on the rolling board and roll it into a thin circle.

3. Smear the top with 2.5 ml (¹/₂ tsp) oil, sprinkle with dry flour and fold in half to create a half moon shape.

4. Again smear the top with oil, sprinkle on the dry flour and fold. Roll out thinly into a triangle shape about 3 mm (¹/₈ in) thick.

5.   Heat the oil in a deep frying pan over a medium-low heat. Slip 4-5 papries gently into the hot oil from the edge of the pan.

6.   Keep turning them over and fry until light brown and crispy. Roll the papries for the next batch while one batch is frying.

Serving suggestion

Serve as it is at tea, or serve it as a 'Chat'. Place 15 ml (1 tbsp) of boiled chickpeas on to it. Pour 15 ml (1 tbsp) whisked natural (plain) yogurt and 5 ml (1 tsp) tamarind chutney over it. Sprinkle over garam masala, red chilli and ground roasted cumin and eat at once before it becomes soggy.

Papri will keep for a fortnight in an airtight tin or container.

Cooking time 14 minutes.

ALOO BONDA
Potato Dumplings

This is one of the simplest, quickest and tastiest ways of using potato in a tea-time snack. You will find this snack to be of medium hotness.

Serves 2	Metric	Imperial	American
For the potato balls			
Potatoes, boiled in jackets, peeled and mashed	250 g	9 oz	9 oz
Green coriander (cilantro) leaves, chopped	15 ml	1 tbsp	1 tbsp
Lemon juice	15 ml	1 tbsp	1 tbsp
Garam masala	2.5 ml	$1/2$ tsp	$1/2$ tsp
Ground red chilli	1.25 ml	$1/4$ tsp	$1/4$ tsp
Small onion, finely chopped	1	1	1
Small green chilli, finely chopped	1	1	1
Salt to taste			
For the batter			
Gram flour, sifted	25 g	1 oz	$1/4$ cup
Oil	5 ml	1 tsp	1 tsp
Tymol seeds (ajwain), cleaned	2.5 ml	$1/2$ tsp	$1/2$ tsp
Salt, to taste			
Water, lukewarm	60 ml	2 tbsp	2 tbsp
Oil for frying			

1.   Place the ingredients for the potato balls in a bowl. Mix thoroughly. Divide the mixture into 6 equal portions, shape into balls and set them to one side.

2.   To make the batter place the gram flour in a bowl. Add the oil, tymol seeds and salt and mix well. Gradually add the water and make a smooth runny batter.

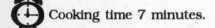

3.   Heat the oil in a deep frying pan over a medium heat.

4.   Dip a potato ball in the batter, making sure that all sides are coated and deep fry all the dumplings. Cook in batches if necessary.

5.   Keep turning them over and fry until golden brown.

6.   Take them out with a slotted spoon and place them on a cooling tray.

Serving suggestions

Serve hot as a starter or at tea-time with chutney, barfi and gulab jamun.

Cooking time 7 minutes.

PAKORA
(Onion and vegetables)
Onion Bhaji

Some Asian restaurants in the U.K. sell the pakora under the name of onion bhaji which is really a misuse of the name. It is one of the delicious snacks which is eaten in every part of India at tea-time. One can make the pakoras with one vegetable only or a mixture of vegetables.

Makes 8 (large)	Metric	Imperial	American
For the batter			
Gram flour, sifted	*100 g*	*4 oz*	*1 cups*
Green coriander (cilantro)			
leaves, chopped	*10 ml*	*2 tsp*	*2 tsp*
Oil	*15 ml*	*1 tbsp*	*1 tbsp*
Garam masala	*5 ml*	*1 tsp*	*1 tsp*
Ground red chilli	*2.5 ml*	*$^1/_2$ tsp*	*$^1/_2$ tsp*
Tymol seeds (ajwain),			
cleaned	*2.5 ml*	*$^1/_2$ tsp*	*$^1/_2$ tsp*
Small green chilli, chopped	*1*	*1*	*1*
Salt, to taste			
Water, lukewarm	*100 ml*	*$3^1/_2$ fl oz*	*$6^1/_2$ tbsp*
For onion and vegetable			
mixture			
Medium onion, thinly sliced	*1*	*1*	*1*
Spinach, chopped	*15 ml*	*1 tbsp*	*1 tbsp*
Medium potato, peeled and			
grated	*1*	*1*	*1*

To make the batter

1.   Place the sifted flour in a bowl and rub in the oil. Add all the remaining ingredients except the water.

2. Gradually pour in the water to make a thick batter. Set the bowl on one side while you cut the vegetables and onion.

3. Mix the onion, spinach and potato together and add to the batter.

4. Heat the oil in a deep frying pan over a medium heat.

5. Put 15 ml (1 tbsp) mixture into the hot oil and fry 7 or 8 pakoras together.

6. When they are lightly brown keep pressing and turning them over until they are cooked and golden brown on all sides.

Serving suggestions

Serve hot at tea-time with tamarind or dhaniya chutney, gulab jamun and barfi. If any pakoras are left over, I reheat them under the grill the next day, wrap them in a slice of bread or chapati and enjoy eating them with a cup of tea.

 Cooking time 15 minutes.

QUICK DALMOD
Quick Bombay Mix

The traditional Bombay mix takes a very long time to cook and requires special equipment. However, so that you have an opportunity to enjoy this delicious snack, I have devised a quick version. The following recipe will half fill a large biscuit tin and should last about a fortnight, although my two children usually finish the whole lot within two days.

Serves 4-6	Metric	Imperial	American
Kellogg's Variety Pack (20 g/ ³/₄ oz mini packets of 1 Corn Pops, 1 Rice Krispies, 1 Banana Bubbles, 2 Frosties, 1 Cornflakes, 1 Cocopops, 1 Honeynut Loops)			
Oil for frying			
Cashew nuts	150 g	5 oz	1¹/₄ cups
Fresh peanuts, shelled	250 g	9 oz	2¹/₄ cups
Oil	15 ml	1 tbsp	1 tbsp
Mustard seeds	5 ml	1 tsp	1 tsp
Aniseed (sonf)	15 ml	1 tbsp	1 tbsp
Whole coriander (cilantro)	15 ml	1 tbsp	1 tbsp
Garam masala	5 ml	1 tsp	1 tsp
Ground red chilli	2.5 ml	¹/₂ tsp	¹/₂ tsp
Salt, to taste			
Sugar	15 ml	1 tbsp	1 tbsp
Raisins	200 g	7 oz	1¹/₄ cups
Citric acid	5 ml	1 tsp	1 tsp

1.   Empty the packets of cereals into a large bowl.

2. Place the oil in a deep frying pan over a medium heat and fry the cashew nuts until light golden brown. Remove from the pan and put them into the bowl.

3. Fry the shelled peanuts until crispy and golden brown. Take them out and put them in the bowl.

4. Heat 15 ml (1 tbsp) oil in a large heavy-bottomed saucepan to make the tarka.

5. Add the mustard seeds and when they start cracking, stir in the aniseed, coriander, garam masala, red chilli, salt, sugar and raisins. Reduce the heat and cook for a further 1 minute. Remove from the heat.

6. While still hot mix in the citric acid.

7. Add the tarka to the large bowl and mix thoroughly.

Preservation

When cold keep in an airtight container. It will keep for up to a fortnight.

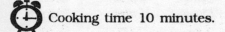 Cooking time 10 minutes.

UPMA
Speciality of South India

This is a very simple nourishing dish from Southern India. In the South most people like to eat hot food. If you want to make your dish hot, increase the quantity of green chilli. Use any vegetable of your choice in place of the peas and corn, if you prefer. You will find this dish to be of medium hotness.

Serves 2	Metric	Imperial	American
Semolina (cream of wheat)	50 g	2 oz	$^1/_3$ cup
Ghee or oil	15 ml	1 tbsp	1 tbsp
Mustard seeds	2.5 ml	$^1/_2$ tsp	$^1/_2$ tsp
Small onion, finely chopped	1	1	1
Fresh ginger, finely chopped	5 mm	$^1/_4$ in	$^1/_4$ in
Garam masala	2.5 ml	$^1/_2$ tsp	$^1/_2$ tsp
Ground red chilli	1.25 ml	$^1/_4$ tsp	$^1/_4$ tsp
Salt, to taste			
Frozen peas	50 g	2 oz	$^1/_2$ cup
Frozen sweetcorn (corn)	50 g	2 oz	$^1/_2$ cup
Milk	120 ml	4 fl oz	$^1/_2$ cup
Water	120 ml	4 fl oz	$^1/_2$ cup
Lemon juice	15 ml	1 tbsp	1 tbsp
Green coriander (cilantro) leaves, finely chopped	10 ml	2 tsp	2 tsp
Small green chilli, finely chopped	1	1	1

1. Cook the semolina in a saucepan until lightly brown over a medium heat for 2 minutes stirring frequently.

2. Heat the ghee in a heavy-bottomed saucepan or deep frying pan. Add the mustard seeds, when they start to crackle put in the onion and ginger and fry them all until lightly brown.

3.   Stir in the garam masala, red chilli, salt, peas and sweetcorn.

4.   Pour in the milk and water and bring to the boil.

5.   Mix in the roasted semolina and stir continuously until all the liquid has been absorbed and the mixture thickens.

6.   Add the lemon juice, coriander leaves and green chilli. Mix thoroughly and serve.

Serving suggestions

Serve hot with coconut chutney and coriander and mint rayta.

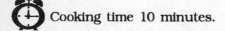 Cooking time 10 minutes.

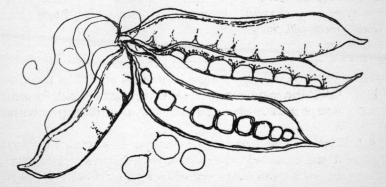

PHAL KI CHAT
Fruit Chat

Chat is sold all over India. Hawkers prepare freshly made chat and sell it on the streets. It is served on large, dried leaves and eaten with sticks (nowadays toothpicks). Chat combines sweet and sour flavours. Fruit chat makes an excellent starter, although at home we prefer to have it after a meal or as a refreshing snack on a hot day.

Serves 4	Metric	Imperial	American
Apples, cut into 2.5 cm (1 in) pieces	1	1	1
Pears, cut into 2.5 cm (1 in) pieces	1	1	1
Guavas, washed and cut into 2.5 cm (1 in) pieces	1	1	1
Grapes, preferably seedless	25 g	1 oz	1 oz
Banana, peeled and cut into 5 mm (^{1}/4 in) rounds	2	2	2
Lemon juice	15 ml	1 tbsp	1 tbsp
Sugar	5 ml	1 tsp	1 tsp
Ground red chilli	small pinch	small pinch	small pinch
Salt, to taste			

1. Place all the above ingredients in a bowl. Mix together and serve cold. Other fruits which can be used for chat are pineapple, orange, papaya, apricot, kiwi, peach and melon, etc.

CURRIES

Think of Indian cuisine and most people will think of curries. In the following section there is something to appeal to everyone. Using traditional spices the curries have an authentic flavour, yet they are quick and easy to prepare.

In India large numbers of people are vegetarian and many different varieties of vegetables are grown. Because of this lots of research has been done into vegetable cookery. Even non-vegetarians do not eat meat every day either because meat is expensive to buy or because it is so hot that people choose not to eat meat daily.

BÉNGUN AUR ALOO
Aubergine and Potato

Aubergines are used in a great many Indian dishes. The following recipe is cooked in the west Indian style. You will find this dish to be of medium hotness.

Serves 2-3	Metric	Imperial	American
Oil	60 ml	4 tbsp	4 tbsp
Mustard seeds	2.5 ml	$^1/_2$ tsp	$^1/_2$ tsp
Cumin seeds	2.5 ml	$^1/_2$ tsp	$^1/_2$ tsp
Large onion, finely chopped	1	1	1
Large garlic cloves, crushed	2	2	2
Fresh ginger, finely chopped	5 mm	$^1/_2$ in	$^1/_2$ in
Coconut, fresh or desiccated	15 ml	2 tbsp	2 tbsp
Potato, peeled and cut into 2.5 cm (1 in) pieces	225 g	8 oz	8 oz
Aubergine, (eggplant) cut into 2.5 cm (1 in) pieces	225 g	8 oz	8 oz
Garam masala	5 ml	1 tsp	1 tsp
Ground coriander (cilantro)	5 ml	1 tsp	1 tsp
Ground red chilli	2.5 ml	$^1/_2$ tsp	$^1/_2$ tsp
Ground turmeric	1.5 ml	$^1/_4$ tsp	$^1/_4$ tsp
Salt, to taste			
Can tomatoes	230 g	8 oz	8 oz
Lemon juice	30 ml	2 tbsp	2 tbsp
Sugar (or jaggery)	15 ml	1 tbsp	1 tbsp
Green coriander (cilantro) leaves, chopped	10 ml	2 tsp	2 tsp
Green chilli, chopped	1	1	1

1. Heat the oil in a large heavy-bottomed saucepan over a medium heat. Add the mustard seeds and when they start to crackle, add the cumin seeds and brown.

2. Put in the onion, garlic and ginger and fry them until lightly brown.

3. Add the potato pieces and fry for 5 minutes or until light brown.

4. Mix in the coconut and aubergine and fry for 2 minutes.

5. Stir in the ground spices and tomatoes, cover the pan and cook for 10 minutes on medium-low heat, stirring occasionally.

6. When the vegetables are tender and all the liquid has been absorbed (the oil will appear on top of the mixture - it may be necessary to increase the heat to do this), add the lemon juice and sugar and cook for a further 2 minutes.

7. Mix in the coriander leaves and green chilli.

Serving suggestions

Serve hot with dal, plain rice, rayta and chapati or paratha.

Cooking time 30 minutes.

CHOTÉ SABAT BENGUN
Baby Aubergines

Chote sabat bengun is one of the best aubergine dishes. Everyone loves this dish in my family except my father who is very choosy about vegetables. I vividly remember the time when Binu, my youngest brother aged two years, was grabbing the baby aubergines with his little hands and the mixture went all over his face and onto his clothes. Father was annoyed and said 'You haven't got any brains because you eat too many benguns and the benguns are 'begun' (Hindi word meaning worthless)'. Binu replied innocently 'Hurry up and give me one penny and I'll buy a brain from the corner sweet shop'. Poor father could not hide his smile and the rest of the family burst into laughter. Do not take father's words too seriously because the aubergines are delicious, and a valuable source of iron.

Serves 2	Metric	Imperial	American
Baby aubergines (eggplant)	250 g	9 oz	9 oz
Oil	60 ml	4 tbsp	4 tbsp
Mustard seeds	2.5 ml	$^1/_2$ tsp	$^1/_2$ tsp
Medium onion, finely chopped	1	1	1
Large garlic cloves, crushed	2	2	2
Fresh ginger, finely chopped	1 cm	$^1/_2$ in	$^1/_2$ in
Garam masala	5 ml	1 tsp	1 tsp
Ground coriander (cilantro)	5 ml	1 tsp	1 tsp
Ground roasted cumin	5 ml	1 tsp	1 tsp
Ground red chilli	1.5 ml	$^1/_4$ tsp	$^1/_4$ tsp
Ground turmeric	1.5 ml	$^1/_4$ tsp	$^1/_4$ tsp
Salt to taste			
Can tomatoes	400 g	14 oz	14 oz
Lemon juice	30 ml	2 tbsp	2 tbsp
Green coriander (cilantro) leaves, chopped	10 ml	2 tsp	2 tsp
Green chilli, chopped	1	1	1

1. Slice the baby aubergines in quarters lengthwise so that the four quarters remain attached to the stalk.

2. Heat the oil in a deep frying pan on medium heat. Add mustard seed and fry until they crackle which will take only seconds.

3. Put in the onion, garlic and ginger and fry until golden brown.

4. Stir in the ground spices, aubergine and tomatoes. Cover the pan and cook for 10 minutes stirring occasionally.

5. Uncover the pan and cook until the aubergines are tender, all the liquid has been absorbed and the oil appears on the top of the mixture.

6. Add the lemon juice and cook for a further 2 minutes. Mix in the coriander leaves and green chilli.

Serving suggestions

Serve hot with any bread, urud or white split moong lentils and rayta.

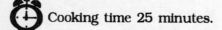 Cooking time 25 minutes.

CHOTÉ BHUTÉ
Baby Sweetcorn Cobs

This delightful dish is prepared from canned baby sweetcorn (corn) cobs. It is very easy to prepare. You will find this dish to be of medium hotness.

Serves 2	Metric	Imperial	American
Can baby sweetcorn (corn) cobs	430 g	15 oz	15 oz
Oil	60 ml	4 tbsp	4 tbsp
Mustard seeds	2.5 ml	$^1/_2$ tsp	$^1/_2$ tsp
Cumin seeds	2.5 ml	$^1/_2$ tsp	$^1/_2$ tsp
Medium onion, finely chopped	1	1	1
Large garlic cloves, crushed	2	2	2
Fresh ginger, finely chopped	1 cm	$^1/_2$ in	$^1/_2$ in
Ground coriander (cilantro)	5 ml	1 tsp	1 tsp
Garam masala	5 ml	1 tsp	1 tsp
Ground red chilli	2.5 ml	$^1/_2$ tsp	$^1/_2$ tsp
Ground turmeric	1.5 ml	$^1/_4$ tsp	$^1/_4$ tsp
Can tomatoes	230 g	8 oz	8 oz
Lemon juice	15 ml	1 tbsp	1 tbsp
Sugar	10 ml	2 tsp	2 tsp
Salt, to taste			

1. Drain the tin of baby corn cobs through a sieve and rinse with cold water.

2. Heat the oil in a heavy-bottomed saucepan on medium heat. Add the mustard seeds and when they start to crackle add the cumin seeds.

3. After a few seconds, put in onion, garlic and ginger and fry until golden brown.

4. Stir in the spices, tomatoes and then the baby corn cobs.

5. Cook until all the liquid has been absorbed and the oil appears on the surface of the mixture.

6. Pour in the lemon juice and mix in the sugar. Stir and turn the heat off when the sugar dissolves.

Serving suggestions

Serve hot with chapati or puri, moong dal, dhaniya chutney and rayta.

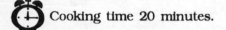 Cooking time 20 minutes.

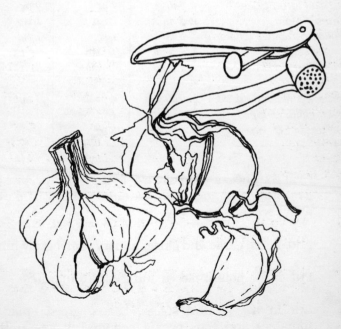

SÉM AUR ALOO KI SABJI

Bean and Potato Curry

In the north of India, beans and potatoes are cooked with onion, tomato and spices which gives them a lovely flavour. In southern India, people like to add coconut milk to the dish instead of tomato. This dish is of medium hotness.

Serves 2	Metric	Imperial	American
Ghee or oil	60 ml	4 tbsp	4 tbsp
Cumin seeds	2.5 ml	1/2 tsp	1/2 tsp
Small onion, finely chopped	1	1	1
Large garlic cloves, crushed	2	2	2
Fresh ginger, finely chopped	1 cm	1/2 in	1/2 in
Potatoes, peeled and cut into 1 cm (1/2 in) pieces	250 g	9 oz	9 oz
Garam masala	5 ml	1 tsp	1 tsp
Ground coriander (cilantro)	5 ml	1 tsp	1 tsp
Ground red chilli	1.5 ml	1/4 tsp	1/4 tsp
Ground turmeric	1.5 ml	1/4 tsp	1/4 tsp
Salt, to taste			
Frozen beans, thawed	100 g	4 oz	1 cup
Green chilli, chopped	1	1	1
Can tomatoes, crushed	230 g	8 oz	8 oz

1. Heat the ghee or oil in a heavy-bottomed saucepan over a medium heat and brown the cumin, this will take only a few seconds.

2. Add onion, garlic and ginger and fry until lightly brown.

3. Put in the potato pieces and fry for 5 minutes.

4. Stir in the ground spices, beans, green chilli and tomatoes and cook over a medium-low heat until all the liquid has been absorbed and the oil appears at the top of the mixture.

5.   Cook for a few minutes longer if the vegetables are not
      tender.

Serving suggestions

Serve hot with onion paratha, chapati, baby corn cobs,
rice and rayta.

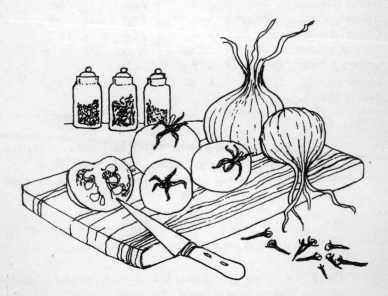 Cooking time 20 minutes.

PIYAJ WALE KARELA

Bitter-Gourd with Onion

This is one of the easiest, simplest and quickest ways of cooking bitter-gourd. This dish is delicious, a little crunchy and it can be kept in the refrigerator for a week.

Indians believe that bitter-gourd cleans the blood. My mother used to say that if you rub bitter-gourd or orange peel on our face and leave it for 30 minutes to an hour, it will make our skin smooth and cure acne.

Serves 2	Metric	Imperial	American
Bitter-gourd, scrape and cut them into rounds 5 mm ($^1/_4$ in) thick	250g	9 oz	9 oz
Oil	60 ml	4 tbsp	4 tbsp
Small onion, thinly sliced	4	4	4
Garam masala	5 ml	1 tsp	1 tsp
Ground coriander (cilantro)	5 ml	1 tsp	1 tsp
Ground roasted cumin	5 ml	1 tsp	1 tsp
Ground red chilli	2.5 ml	$^1/_2$ tsp	$^1/_2$ tsp
Ground turmeric	1.25 ml	$^1/_4$ tsp	$^1/_4$ tsp
Lemon juice	15 ml	1 tbsp	1 tbsp
Salt, to taste			

1. Boil the bitter-gourd in salt water for 1 minute. When cool, boil the vegetable again. This time when the gourd is cold, drain it and squeeze out the excess moisture with the palm of your hand.

2. Heat the oil in a flat or deep frying pan over a medium heat. Add onion and fry until light brown.

3. Put in the bitter-gourd and fry for 15-20 minutes until golden brown and crispy. Do not allow the gourd to cook too quickly.

4. Stir in the spices and cook for a further 2-3 minutes on low heat. Add the lemon juice and salt to taste.

Serving suggestions

Serve hot or cold with chapati, paratha or puri, moong or urud dal, rice and rayta.

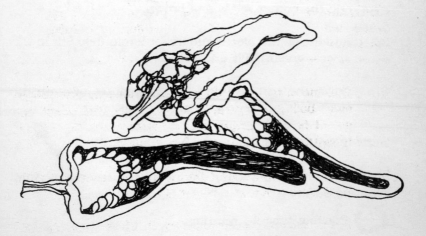 Cooking time 25 minutes.

BROCCOLI AND POTATO

You will find this dish to be of medium hotness.

Serves 2	Metric	Imperial	American
Broccoli, cut into florets	250 g	9 oz	9 oz
Potatoes, peeled and cut into 1 cm ($\frac{1}{2}$ in) pieces	250 g	9 oz	9 oz
Oil	60 ml	4 tbsp	4 tbsp
Mustard seeds	5 ml	1 tsp	1 tsp
Cumin	5 ml	1 tsp	1 tsp
Garam masala	5 ml	1 tsp	1 tsp
Ground coriander (cilantro)	5 ml	1 tsp	1 tsp
Ground red chilli	1.5 ml	$\frac{1}{4}$ tsp	$\frac{1}{4}$ tsp
Ground turmeric	1.5 ml	$\frac{1}{4}$ tsp	$\frac{1}{4}$ tsp
Salt, to taste			
Green chilli, chopped	1	1	1

1. Heat the oil in a deep frying pan over a medium heat. Add the mustard seeds and when they start crackling add the cumin seeds and brown.

2. Add the potato pieces and fry for 2 minutes. Stir in the spices, green chilli and broccoli.

3. Cover the pan and cook for 12 minutes or until the vegetables are tender, stirring occasionally.

Serving suggestions

Serve hot with moong dal, rayta, chutney and chapati or puri.

 Cooking time 14 minutes.

FRIED BHINDI OR OKRA
Lady's Fingers (North Indian Style)

Do not be put off by the sticky nature of fresh okra when cooked in the following way, bhindi is delicious and crispy.

Serves 2	Metric	Imperial	American
Oil	60 ml	4 tbsp	4 tbsp
Medium onion, finely chopped	1	1	1
Tender lady's fingers, ends trimmed and cut into 1 cm ($^1/_2$ in) round pieces	225 g	8 oz	8 oz
Ground coriander (cilantro)	5 ml	1 tsp	1 tsp
Ground roasted cumin	2.5 ml	$^1/_2$ tsp	$^1/_2$ tsp
Ground turmeric	1.5 ml	$^1/_4$ tsp	$^1/_4$ tsp
Ground red chilli	2.5 ml	$^1/_2$ tsp	$^1/_2$ tsp
Garam masala	2.5 ml	$^1/_2$ tsp	$^1/_2$ tsp
Small green chilli, finely chopped	1	1	1
Salt, to taste			

1. Heat the oil in a frying pan over a medium heat and lightly brown the onion. Add the okra pieces, cover with a lid and cook for a further 5 minutes.

2. Stir in the coriander, ground spices, green chilli and salt. Cook over a low heat for a further 5-7 minutes or until tender. Keep turning the okra over until cooked.

Serving suggestion

Serve hot with paratha or puri, dal, rayta and rice.

Cooking time 15 minutes.

GAJAR - MATAR KI SABJI

Carrot and Peas (North Indian Style)

This nourishing vegetable dish is cooked differently in every part of India. In the west of India, onion and garlic are avoided and lemon and sugar are added instead. You will find this dish to be of medium hotness.

Serves 2	Metric	Imperial	American
Oil	*60 ml*	*4 tbsp*	*4 tbsp*
Small onion, finely chopped	*1*	*1*	*1*
Large garlic cloves, crushed	*2*	*2*	*2*
Fresh ginger, finely chopped	*1 cm*	*$^1/_2$ in*	*$^1/_2$ in*
Ground coriander (cilantro)	*5 ml*	*1 tsp*	*1 tsp*
Garam masala	*5 ml*	*1 tsp*	*1 tsp*
Ground red chilli	*1.5 ml*	*$^1/_4$ tsp*	*$^1/_4$ tsp*
Ground turmeric	*1.5 ml*	*$^1/_4$ tsp*	*$^1/_4$ tsp*
Salt to taste			
Can tomatoes	*230 g*	*8 oz*	*8 oz*
Tender small carrots, cut into 2.5 cm (1 in) pieces.	*250 g*	*9 oz*	*9 oz*
Fresh peas, shelled or frozen peas, thawed	*100 g*	*4 oz*	*4 oz*
Green coriander leaves, (cilantro) chopped	*10 ml*	*2 tsp*	*2 tsp*
Small green chilli, chopped	*1*	*1*	*1*

1. Heat the oil in a large heavy-bottomed saucepan. Add the onion, garlic and the ginger and fry gently over a medium heat until golden brown.

2. Stir in the coriander, garam masala, red chilli, turmeric and salt, followed by the tomatoes and the carrots.

3. Cover with the lid, reduce the heat to medium-low. Cook for 10 minutes or until carrot pieces are tender, stirring occasionally.

4. Increase the heat and mix in the peas. Cook for a further few minutes until the peas are tender and the oil appears on the surface of the mixture.

5. Stir in the green coriander leaves and green chilli.

Serving suggestions

Serve hot with dal, rice, puri and rayta.

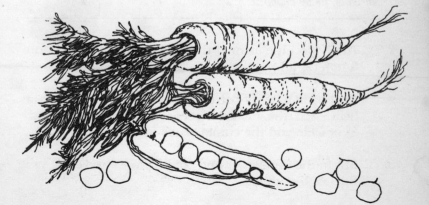 Cooking time 25 minutes.

GOBHI ALOO

Cauliflower and Potato

This is one of my simplest and easiest cauliflower dishes to prepare and it takes very little time as well. It is of medium hotness.

Serves 2-3	Metric	Imperial	American
Small cauliflower, cut into 2.5 cm (1 in) florets,	1	1	1
Potato, peeled and cut into 1 cm ($^1/_2$ in) pieces	225 g	8 oz	8 oz
Oil	60 ml	4 tbsp	4 tbsp
Mustard seeds	2.5 ml	$^1/_2$ tsp	$^1/_2$ tsp
Cumin seeds	5 ml	1 tsp	1 tsp
Ground coriander (cilantro)	10 ml	2 tsp	2 tsp
Garam masala	5 ml	1 tsp	1 tsp
Ground red chilli	2.5 ml	$^1/_2$ tsp	$^1/_2$ tsp
Ground turmeric	2.5 ml	$^1/_2$ tsp	$^1/_2$ tsp
Salt to taste			
Coriander (cilantro) leaves, finely chopped	10 ml	2 tsp	2 tsp
Green chilli, finely chopped	1	1	1

1.   Thinly peel the stem of the cauliflower and cut it into 5 mm (¼ in) rounds.

2.   Heat oil in a heavy-bottomed saucepan over a medium heat. Add the mustard seeds and when they start to crackle add the cumin seeds and brown.

3.   Stir in the cauliflower and potato pieces and cook for a further 5 minutes.

4. Stir in the ground spices and place the lid on the pan. Steam cook until the vegetables are tender. Make sure you stir the dish from time to time. If the cauliflower is not fresh you may have to sprinkle with water occasionally, though steam cooked cauliflower tastes better.

5. When the cauliflower and potato pieces are cooked add green coriander leaves and green chilli, and stir.

Serving suggestions

Serve hot with puri or any other bread, white split moong lentils, rayta and rice.

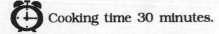 Cooking time 30 minutes.

KHATÉWALÉ KABULI CHANNA
Chickpeas

This popular dish is prepared in the Punjabi style. Chickpeas take a long time to cook, so I used canned chickpeas which will enable you to cook the dish in 15 minutes. You will find this dish to be of medium hotness.

Serves 2-3	Metric	Imperial	American
Can chickpeas	410 g	14 ¹/₂ oz	14 ¹/₂ oz
Oil	60 ml	4 tbsp	4 tbsp
Cumin seeds	2.5 ml	¹/₂ tsp	¹/₂ tsp
Medium onion, finely chopped	1	1	1
Large garlic cloves, chopped	2	2	2
Fresh ginger	1 cm	¹/₂ in	¹/₂ in
Ground coriander (cilantro)	5 ml	1 tsp	1 tsp
Garam masala	5 ml	1 tsp	1 tsp
Ground roasted cumin	5 ml	1 tsp	1 tsp
Ground red chilli	2.5 ml	¹/₂ tsp	¹/₂ tsp
Ground turmeric	1.5 ml	¹/₄ tsp	¹/₄ tsp
Salt, to taste			
Can tomatoes	230 g	8 oz	8 oz
Tamarind pulp (see the recipe on page 18)	25 g	1 oz	2 tbsp
Green chilli	1	1	1
Green coriander (cilantro) leaves, finely chopped	15 ml	1 tbsp	1 tbsp

1.   Drain and rinse the chickpeas.

2.   Heat the oil in a heavy-bottomed saucepan. Add the cumin seeds which will take 2 seconds to brown. Add the onion, garlic and ginger and fry over a medium heat until golden brown.

3. Mix in the ground spices and the tomatoes. Cook until all the liquid has been absorbed and the oil appears on the top of the mixture.

4. Stir in the chickpeas and tamarind pulp. Simmer for 2 minutes.

5. Add the green chilli and coriander leaves. Stir and turn off the heat.

Serving suggestion

Serve it hot with puri, rayta, tamarind chutney and puri wale aloo.

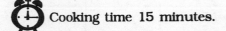 Cooking time 15 minutes.

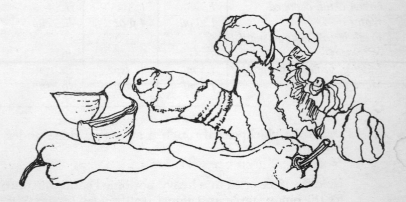

CHICKPEAS IN SAUCE
(North India-Punjabi Style)

This delicious dish is very popular in the Punjab. During the hot summer days in India, when we do not want to eat very much, chickpeas in sauce with plain rice, rayta and pickle will stimulate our appetite.

Serves 2	Metric	Imperial	American
Can chickpeas	410 g	14 1/2 oz	14 1/2 oz
Ghee or oil	60 ml	4 tbsp	4 tbsp
Large onion, finely chopped	1	1	1
Large garlic cloves, crushed	2	2	2
Fresh ginger, finely chopped	1 cm	1/2 in	1/2 in
Garam masala	5 ml	1 tsp	1 tsp
Ground coriander (cilantro)	5 ml	1 tsp	1 tsp
Roasted cumin	2.5 ml	1/2 tsp	1/2 tsp
Ground red chilli	1.5 ml	1/4 tsp	1/4 tsp
Ground turmeric	1.5 ml	1/4 tsp	1/4 tsp
Salt, to taste			
Can tomatoes, crushed	230 g	8 oz	8 oz
Coriander (cilantro) leaves, chopped	10 ml	2 tsp	2 tsp
Green chilli, chopped	1	1	1
Water	120 ml	4 fl oz	1/2 cup
Fresh lemon, cut into small pieces	1/2	1/2	1/2
Nutmeg, grated (optional)	1.5 ml	1/4 tsp	1/4 tsp
Mace (optional)	1.5 ml	1/4 tsp	1/4 tsp

1. Drain the chickpeas through a sieve and rinse under the tap.

2. Heat the ghee or oil in a heavy-bottomed saucepan and fry the onion, garlic and ginger until golden brown. Stir in the ground spices, tomatoes and chickpeas. Cook

until all the liquid has been absorbed and the oil appears on the top of the mixture.

3. Sprinkle in the nutmeg and mace and mix in the coriander leaves and green chilli. Pour in the water and bring to the boil. Reduce the heat to low and simmer for 2 minutes.

4. Squeeze the fresh lemon juice over the chickpeas when you are ready to serve them.

Serving suggestions

Serve hot with plain rice, chapati, rayta, fried okra or baby aubergines.

Cooking time 15 minutes.

TUROI BHAJI

Courgette Bhaji ✓

Always choose thin, fresh courgettes because they cook quickly and are sweeter. This dish is of medium hotness.

Serves 2	Metric	Imperial	American
Courgettes (zucchini), sliced	250 g	9 oz	9 oz
Oil	60 ml	4 tbsp	4 tbsp
Mustard seeds	2.5 ml	$^1/_2$ tsp	$^1/_2$ tsp
Small onion, finely chopped	1	1	1
Ground coriander (cilantro)	5 ml	1 tsp	1 tsp
Garam masala	2.5 ml	$^1/_2$ tsp	$^1/_2$ tsp
Ground red chilli	1.5 ml	$^1/_4$ tsp	$^1/_4$ tsp
Ground turmeric	1.5 ml	$^1/_4$ tsp	$^1/_4$ tsp
Salt, to taste			
Can tomatoes	230 g	8 oz	8 oz
Small green chilli, chopped	1	1	1

1. Heat the oil in a deep frying pan over medium heat. Add the mustard seeds and when they start to crackle add the onion and fry until golden brown.

2. Stir in the ground spices, courgette, green chilli and tomatoes. Cover the pan and cook, stirring occasionally for 5 minutes until all the liquid has been absorbed and the oil appears on the surface of the mixture.

3. When the courgette is tender, turn off the heat.

Serving suggestions

Serve hot with chapati, chola dal, plain rice and rayta.

Cooking time 10 minutes.

MASSALÉ DAR SÉM

Spicy Baked Beans

My son always makes this recipe when he is busy finishing his assignments at university. You will find it to be of medium hotness.

Serves 2	Metric	Imperial	American
Can baked beans	450 g	1 lb	1lb
Oil	30 ml	2 tbsp	2tbsp
Small onion, finely chopped	1	1	1
Garam masala	2.5 ml	$^1/_2$ tsp	$^1/_2$ tsp
Ground coriander (cilantro)	2.5 ml	$^1/_2$ tsp	$^1/_2$ tsp
Ground red chilli	1.5 ml	$^1/_4$ tsp	$^1/_4$ tsp
Salt, to taste			

1. Heat the oil in a heavy-bottomed saucepan over a medium heat and fry the onion until light golden brown. Stir in the spices.

2. Mix in the baked beans and bring to the boil. Reduce the heat and simmer for 2-3 minutes so that the spices get a chance to mature.

Serving suggestions

Serve on toast, obviously! You can serve it with any dish.

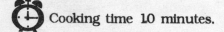 Cooking time 10 minutes.

SUKHĀ SOYA KEEMA AUR MATAR
Dried Soya Mince and Peas

This delicious dish is full of protein and very nutritious. Dried soya mince is available from most supermarkets. You will find this dish to be of medium hotness.

Serves 2	Metric	Imperial	American
Dried soya mince,	25 g	1 oz	1/4 cup
Oil	60 ml	4 tbsp	4 tbsp
Medium onion, finely chopped	1	1	1
Large garlic cloves, crushed	2	2	2
Fresh ginger, finely chopped	1 cm	1/2 in	1/2 in
Garam masala	5 ml	1 tsp	1 tsp
Ground coriander (cilantro)	5 ml	1 tsp	1 tsp
Ground roasted cumin	2.5 ml	1/2 tsp	1/2 tsp
Ground red chilli	1.5 ml	1/4 tsp	1/4 tsp
Ground turmeric	1.5 ml	1/4 tsp	1/4 tsp
Salt, to taste			
Can tomatoes, crushed	230 g	8 oz	8 oz
Frozen peas, thawed	150 g	5 oz	1 1/4 cups
Green coriander (cilantro) leaves, chopped	10 ml	2 tsp	2 tsp
Green chilli, chopped	1	1	1

1. Soak the dried soya mince in boiling water for 10 minutes and drain thoroughly through a sieve.

2. Heat the oil in a heavy-bottomed saucepan over a medium heat. Add the onion, garlic and ginger and fry until golden brown. Mix in the drained soya mince and fry for 1 minute.

3. Stir in the ground spices, tomatoes and peas. Cook until all the liquid has been absorbed and the oil appears on the top of the mixture.

4. Mix in the green coriander leaves and green chilli. Remove from the heat.

Serving suggestions

Serve hot with nan, rayta, pulao and green lentils.

Cooking time 20 minutes.

MÉTHI-ALOO KI SABJ BHAJI
Fenugreek Leaves and Potato

This is a very tasty dish. The fenugreek leaves are very easy to grow but if you have not got fresh leaves then use 30 ml (2 tbsp) dried leaves instead.

Serves 2	Metric	Imperial	American
Fresh fenugreek leaves, bunch	2	2	2
Oil	60 ml	4 tbsp	4 tbsp
Cumin seeds	2.5 ml	1/2 tsp	1/2 tsp
Small onion, finely chopped	1	1	1
Potatoes, peeled and cut into 1 cm (1/2 in) pieces	250 g	9 oz	9 oz
Garam masala	5 ml	1 tsp	1 tsp
Ground coriander (cilantro)	5 ml	1 tsp	1 tsp
Ground red chilli	1.5 ml	1/4 tsp	1/4 tsp
Ground turmeric	large pinch	large pinch	large pinch
Salt, to taste			
Green chilli, chopped	1	1	1

1. Remove the stalks from the fenugreek, only use the leaves and the tender stem. Wash very thoroughly and chop coarsely. If using dried leaves take out the sticks and soak the leaves in lukewarm water for 2 minutes, then lift the leaves out from the top and squeeze out the water.

2. Heat the oil in a deep frying pan and brown the cumin seeds, this will take a few seconds. Add the onion and fry until light brown.

3. Fry the potato pieces until light brown.

4.   Stir in the ground spices, fenugreek leaves and green chilli. Cover the pan and cook over a medium to low heat until the potatoes are tender. Make sure you stir the dish occasionally.

Serving suggestions

Serve hot with chapati or onion paratha, moong or arhar dal and rayta.

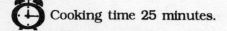 Cooking time 25 minutes.

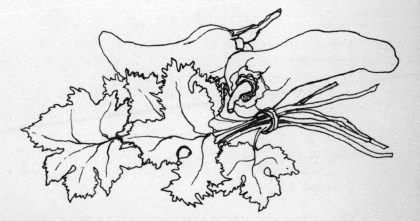

SÉM AUR ALOO

French Beans and Potato

This delightful dish is very popular in the west of India. In this region people like to add a little sugar and lemon to almost all their dishes.

Serves 4	Metric	Imperial	American
Oil	60 ml	4 tbsp	4 tbsp
Mustard seeds	2.5 ml	$^1/_2$ tsp	$^1/_2$ tsp
Cumin seeds	2.5 ml	$^1/_2$ tsp	$^1/_2$ tsp
Large garlic cloves, crushed	2	2	2
Fresh ginger, finely chopped	1 cm	$^1/_2$ in	$^1/_2$ in
Potatoes, peeled, cut into 1 cm ($^1/_2$ in) pieces	250 g	9 oz	9 oz
French (green) beans, ends trimmed, string removed, cut into 1 cm ($^1/_2$ in) pieces	150 g	5 oz	5 oz
Garam masala	5 ml	1 tsp	1 tsp
Ground coriander (cilantro)	5 ml	1 tsp	1 tsp
Ground roasted cumin	2.5 ml	$^1/_2$ tsp	$^1/_2$ tsp
Ground red chilli	1.5 ml	$^1/_4$ tsp	$^1/_4$ tsp
Ground turmeric	1.5 ml	$^1/_4$ tsp	$^1/_4$ tsp
Salt, to taste			
Green chilli, chopped	1	1	1
Lemon juice	15 ml	1 tbsp	1 tbsp
Sugar	10 ml	2 tsp	2 tsp

1. Heat the oil in a heavy-bottomed saucepan over a medium heat. Add mustard seeds and when they start to crackle, add the cumin seeds and brown, this will take a few seconds.

2. Mix in the garlic, ginger and potato pieces and fry for 5 minutes. Add the beans and fry for a further 2 minutes.

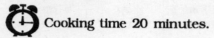

3. Stir in the spices, cover the pan and reduce the heat to medium-low. Cook for 10 minutes or until tender, stirring occasionally.

4. Add the green chilli, lemon juice and sugar and simmer for a further 1-2 minutes.

Serving suggestions

Serve hot with puri or paratha, urud ki sukhi dal, rice and rayta.

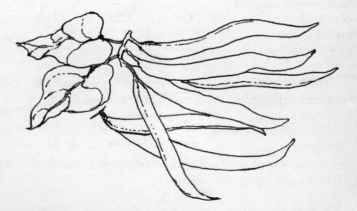

Cooking time 20 minutes.

PAHADI MIRCHA AUR ALOO
Green Pepper and Potato

This is one of the simplest and the easiest ways of cooking green pepper and potatoes. You will find this dish to be of medium hotness.

Serves 2-3	Metric	Imperial	American
Oil	60 ml	4 tbsp	4 tbsp
Mustard seeds	2.5 ml	1/2 tsp	1/2 tsp
Cumin seeds	2.5 ml	1/2 tsp	1/2 tsp
Potatoes, peeled and cut into 1 cm (1/2 in) pieces	250 g	9 oz	9 oz
Garam masala	5 ml	1 tsp	1 tsp
Ground coriander (cilantro)	5 ml	1 tsp	1 tsp
Ground red chilli	1.5 ml	1/4 tsp	1/4 tsp
Ground turmeric	1.5ml	1/4 tsp	1/4 tsp
Salt, to taste			
Medium green (bell) pepper, cut into 2.5 cm (1 in) pieces	1	1	1
Can tomatoes, mashed	230 g	8 oz	8 oz
Green coriander (cilantro) leaves, chopped	10 ml	2 tsp	2 tsp
Green chilli, chopped	1	1	1

1. Heat the oil in a deep frying pan or saucepan over a medium heat. Add mustard seeds and when they start to crackle, brown the cumin seeds, this will take only a few seconds.

2. Mix in the potato pieces and cook for about 5 minutes until lightly brown.

3. Stir in the ground spices, green pepper and tomatoes. Cover the pan and reduce the heat, steam cook for a further 8-9 minutes stirring occasionally, until the vegetables are tender.

4. Mix in the green coriander leaves and green chilli.

Serving suggestions

Serve it hot with urud or moong ki dhuli dal, rice, puri or chapati, rayta and chutney.

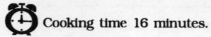 Cooking time 16 minutes.

BHARTA

Mashed Aubergine (North Indian Style)

To make bharta you need large aubergines. In India, 90 per cent of people still use wood or coal for cooking. Aubergines will normally be roasted under hot ashes, cooking this way adds extra flavour. You will find this dish to be of medium hotness.

Serves 2-3	Metric	Imperial	American
Oil	60 ml	4 tbsp	4 tbsp
Mustard seeds	2.5 ml	$^1/_2$ tsp	$^1/_2$ tsp
Cumin seeds	2.5 ml	$^1/_2$ tsp	$^1/_2$ tsp
Medium onion, finely chopped	1	1	1
Fresh ginger, finely chopped	5 mm	$^1/_4$ in	$^1/_4$ in
Large aubergine (eggplant)	250 g	9 oz	9 oz
Garam masala	5 ml	1 tsp	1 tsp
Ground coriander (cilantro)	5 ml	1 tsp	1 tsp
Ground red chilli	1.5 ml	$^1/_4$ tsp	$^1/_4$ tsp
Ground turmeric	1.5 ml	$^1/_4$ tsp	$^1/_4$ tsp
Can tomatoes, mashed	230 g	8 oz	8 oz
Green coriander (cilantro) leaves, chopped	10 ml	2 tsp	2 tsp
Salt, to taste			
Small green chilli, chopped	1	1	1

1. Grill (broil) the aubergine on all sides until the skin begins to blister. Remove from the heat, cool, peel and mash.

2. Heat the oil in a heavy-bottomed saucepan on medium heat. Add the mustard seeds and fry them until they crackle. Add the cumin seeds which will take only 2 seconds to brown.

3. Mix in the onion and ginger and fry gently until lightly browned.

4. Stir in the mashed aubergine and cook for a further 5 minutes.

5. Add the ground spices, salt and the tomatoes. Cook until all the water has been absorbed and the oil appears on the top of the mixture.

6. Mix in the green coriander leaves and green chilli and serve.

Serving suggestions

Serve hot with puri or chapati, rice, dal and rayta.

 Cooking time 15 minutes.

KHUMBI AUR BHUTÉ KÉ DANÉ

Mushroom and Sweetcorn

This is an absolutely delicious dish. When entertaining your friends you may like to add cashew nuts and raisins. You will find this dish to be of medium hotness.

Serves 2	Metric	Imperial	American
Oil	60 ml	4 tbsp	4 tbsp
Mustard seeds	2.5 ml	1/2 tsp	1/2 tsp
Cumin seeds	2.5 ml	1/2 tsp	1/2 tsp
Medium onion, finely chopped	1	1	1
Large garlic cloves	2	2	2
Fresh ginger, finely chopped	5 mm	1/4 in	1/4 in
Mushrooms, trim the stalk and cut into quarters	150 g	5 oz	5 oz
Garam masala	5 ml	1 tsp	1 tsp
Ground coriander (cilantro)	5 ml	1 tsp	1 tsp
Ground red chilli	1.5 ml	1/4 tsp	1/4 tsp
Ground turmeric	2.5 ml	1/2 tsp	1/2 tsp
Frozen sweetcorn (corn), thawed	150 g	5 oz	5 oz
Can tomatoes	230 g	8 oz	8 oz
Green coriander (cilantro) leaves, chopped	10 ml	2 tsp	2 tsp
Small green chilli, finely chopped	1	1	1

1. Heat the oil in a heavy-bottomed saucepan over a medium heat. Add the mustard seeds, when they start to crackle, brown the cumin seeds.

2. Add onion, garlic and ginger and fry until light brown.

3. Put in the mushrooms and fry for a further 5-6 minutes.

4. Stir in the ground spices, sweetcorn and mashed tomatoes. Cook until all the liquid has been absorbed and oil appears on the surface of the mixture.

5. Mix in the green coriander leaves and green chilli.

Serving suggestions

Serve hot with puri, dal, rice and rayta.

 Cooking time 25 minutes.

PURI WALÉ ALOO
Potato Curry

This is a most simple and delicious dish. You will find this dish to be medium hot.

Serves 2	Metric	Imperial	American
Oil or ghee	60 ml	4 tbsp	4 tbsp
Mustard seeds	2.5 ml	$^1/_2$ tsp	$^1/_2$ tsp
Cumin seeds	2.5 ml	$^1/_2$ tsp	$^1/_2$ tsp
Potatoes, boiled in skins, peeled and cut into 5 mm ($^1/_4$ in) pieces	250 g	9 oz	9 oz
Ground coriander (cilantro)	5 ml	1 tsp	1 tsp
Ground roasted cumin	2.5 ml	$^1/_2$ tsp	$^1/_2$ tsp
Garam masala	5 ml	1 tsp	1 tsp
Ground red chilli	1.5 ml	$^1/_4$ tsp	$^1/_4$ tsp
Ground turmeric	1.5 ml	$^1/_4$ tsp	$^1/_4$ tsp
Salt, to taste			
Can tomatoes, crushed	230 g	8 oz	8 oz
Water	120 ml	4 fl oz	$^1/_2$ cup
Lemon juice	15 ml	1 tbsp	1 tbsp
Green coriander (cilantro) leaves, chopped	15 ml	1 tbsp	1 tbsp
Small green chilli, chopped	1	1	1

1. Heat the oil in a heavy-bottomed saucepan. Add the mustard seeds and when they start to crackle, brown the cumin seeds.

2. Mix in the potato pieces and fry them until light brown.

3. Stir in the ground spices, salt and tomatoes. Cook until all the liquid has been absorbed.

4. Pour in the water and bring to the boil. Reduce the heat to low and simmer for 2 minutes. Add the lemon juice and mix in the coriander leaves and green chilli.

Serving suggestions

Serve hot with puri, jalebi, lassi and pickle at any meal.

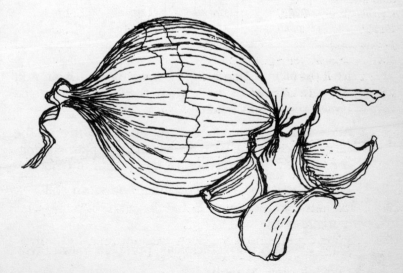 Cooking time 15 minutes.

SITĀPHAL KI SABJI
Pumpkin Ki Sabji

In India there is a festival called 'Kanjka'. Pumpkin is one of the traditional dishes. It is of medium hotness.

Serves 2-3	Metric	Imperial	American
Pumpkin, peeled and cut into 5 mm (¼ in) cubes	*450 g*	*1 lb*	*1 lb*
Oil	*60 ml*	*4 tbsp*	*4 tbsp*
Mustard seeds	*2.5 ml*	*½ tsp*	*½ tsp*
Cumin seeds	*2.5 ml*	*½ tsp*	*½ tsp*
Garam masala	*5 ml*	*1 tsp*	*1 tsp*
Ground coriander (cilantro)	*5 ml*	*1 tsp*	*1 tsp*
Ground red chilli	*1.5 ml*	*¼ tsp*	*¼ tsp*
Ground turmeric	*1.5 ml*	*¼ tsp*	*¼ tsp*
Salt, to taste			
Lemon juice	*15 ml*	*1 tbsp*	*1 tbsp*
Green coriander (cilantro) leaves, chopped	*10 ml*	*2 tsp*	*2 tsp*
Green chilli, chopped	*1*	*1*	*1*

1.   Heat the oil in a deep frying pan over medium heat. Add the mustard seeds and when they start to crackle brown the cumin seeds.

2.   Add the diced pumpkin and ground spices. Reduce the heat and cover the pan. Steam the pumpkin stirring occasionally, for a further 15 minutes until tender.

3.   Mix in the lemon juice, coriander and green chilli.

Serving suggestions

Serve hot with puri, chickpeas, pumpkin halwa rayta.

Cooking time 20 minutes.

Masalé dar Matar

Spicy Peas

This delicious dish is suitable for any meal or serve as a snack with a slice of bread. This dish is of medium hotness.

Serves 2	Metric	Imperial	American
Oil	30 ml	2 tbsp	2 tbsp
Cumin seeds	2.5 ml	$1/2$ tsp	$1/2$ tsp
Garam masala	5 ml	1 tsp	1 tsp
Ground coriander (cilantro)	5 ml	1 tsp	1 tsp
Ground roasted cumin	2.5 ml	$1/2$ tsp	$1/2$ tsp
Ground red chilli	1.5 ml	$1/4$ tsp	$1/4$ tsp
Ground turmeric	1.5 ml	$1/4$ tsp	$1/4$ tsp
Salt to taste			
Frozen peas, thawed	250 g	9 oz	9 oz
Lemon juice	30 ml	2 tbsp	2 tbsp
Green coriander (cilantro) leaves, chopped	15 ml	1 tbsp	1 tbsp
Small green chilli, chopped	1	1	1

1. Heat the oil in a heavy-bottomed saucepan over a medium heat. Add the cumin seeds and brown them. Stir in all the ground spices and the peas. Cover the pan and cook for 5 minutes, stirring from time to time.

2. Pour in the lemon juice and cook for a further 2-3 minutes or until all the liquid has been absorbed. Mix in the green coriander leaves and green chilli.

Serving suggestions

Serve hot with bread or white split moong lentils, plain rice, puri or onion paratha and potato curry.

Cooking time 9 minutes.

RAJMA
Red Kidney Bean

Red kidney beans are one of the best and richest sources of protein, especially for vegetarians, but they take a very long time to cook without a pressure cooker, so I have used canned red kidney beans. Most Punjabies cook this recipe once a week. This dish is of medium hotness.

Serves 2-3	Metric	Imperial	American
Can red kidney beans	410 g	14¹/₂ oz	14¹/₂ oz
Oil	60 ml	4 tbsp	4 tbsp
Medium onion, finely chopped	1	1	1
Large garlic cloves, chopped	2	2	2
Fresh ginger, finely chopped	1 cm	¹/₂ in	¹/₂ in
Ground coriander (cilantro)	5 ml	1 tsp	1 tsp
Garam masala	5 ml	1 tsp	1 tsp
Ground roasted cumin	2.5 ml	¹/₂ tsp	¹/₂ tsp
Ground red chilli	2.5 ml	¹/₂ tsp	¹/₂ tsp
Ground turmeric	1.5 ml	¹/₄ tsp	¹/₄ tsp
Salt, to taste			
Can tomatoes, crushed	230 g	8 oz	8 oz
Small green chilli, finely chopped	1	1	1
Green coriander (cilantro) leaves, finely chopped	15 ml	1 tbsp	1 tbsp
Water	60 ml	4 tbsp	4 tbsp

1. Drain the kidney beans through a sieve and rinse well under the cold water tap.

2. Heat the oil in a heavy-bottomed saucepan and fry the onion, garlic and ginger until golden brown.

3. Stir in the ground spices and mashed tomatoes. Cook until all the liquid has been absorbed and the oil appears on the surface of the mixture. Stir in the drained beans and cook for a further 2 minutes.

4. Pour in water, bring to the boil and simmer for 2 minutes.

5. Sprinkle over chopped green chilli and coriander leaves.

Serving suggestions

Serve hot with plain rice, chapati, cauliflower and rayta.

Cooking time 20 minutes.

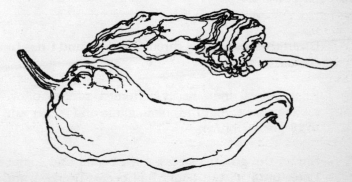

SOYA BEANS

This dish is delicious and full of protein. To reduce the preparation time I used canned soya beans. You will find this dish to be of medium hotness.

Serves 2	Metric	Imperial	American
Medium onion, finely chopped	*1*	*1*	*1*
Large garlic cloves, crushed	*2*	*2*	*2*
Fresh ginger, finely chopped	*1 cm*	*$^1/_2$ in*	*$^1/_2$ in*
Garam masala	*5 ml*	*1 tsp*	*1 tsp*
Ground coriander (cilantro)	*5 ml*	*1 tsp*	*1 tsp*
Ground red chilli	*1.5 ml*	*$^1/_4$ tsp*	*$^1/_4$ tsp*
Ground turmeric	*1.5 ml*	*$^1/_4$ tsp*	*$^1/_4$ tsp*
Salt, to taste			
Can soya beans	*410 g*	*14$^1/_2$ oz*	*14$^1/_2$ oz*
Oil or ghee	*60 ml*	*4 tbsp*	*4 tbsp*
Can tomatoes, crushed	*230 g*	*8 oz*	*8 oz*
Water	*120 ml*	*4 fl oz*	*$^1/_2$ cup*
Green coriander (cilantro) leaves, chopped	*10 ml*	*2 tsp*	*2 tsp*
Small green chilli, chopped	*1*	*1*	*1*

1. Drain the soya beans through a sieve and rinse under the cold water tap.

2. Heat the oil in a heavy-bottomed saucepan over a medium heat. Add the onion, garlic and ginger and fry until golden brown.

3. Stir in the ground spices, soya beans and tomatoes. Cook until all the liquid has been absorbed and oil appears on the top of the mixture.

4. Add water, bring to the boil, reduce heat to low and simmer for 2 minutes. Mix in the coriander leaves and green chilli.

Serving suggestions

Serve hot with plain rice, spicy peas, rayta and chapati.

 Cooking time 15 minutes.

PALK PANEER

Spinach and Indian Cheese (North Indian Style)

This is a superb dish, especially for vegetarians. It has a very high food value and is full of protein, iron and many minerals. It is a delicious party dish, but I like to cook it at least once a week because my family love it. You will find this dish to be of medium hotness.

Serves 2	Metric	Imperial	American
Oil or ghee	*60 ml*	*4 tbsp*	*4 tbsp*
Medium onion, finely chopped	*1*	*1*	*1*
Large garlic cloves, crushed	*2*	*2*	*2*
Fresh ginger, finely chopped	*1 cm*	*¹/₂ in*	*¹/₂ in*
Ground coriander (cilantro)	*5 ml*	*1 tsp*	*1 tsp*
Garam masala	*5 ml*	*1 tsp*	*1 tsp*
Ground roasted cumin	*2.5 ml*	*¹/₂ tsp*	*¹/₂ tsp*
Ground red chilli	*2.5 ml*	*¹/₂ tsp*	*¹/₂ tsp*
Ground turmeric	*1.5 ml*	*¹/₄ tsp*	*¹/₄ tsp*
Salt to taste			
Can tomatoes	*230 g*	*8 oz*	*8 oz*
Frozen spinach, thawed and finely chopped	*150 g*	*5 oz*	*5 oz*
Paneer (see page 16), use 1.2 l/ 2 pt/ 5 cups milk cut into 1 cm (¹/₂ in) squares	*150 g*	*5 oz*	*5 oz*
Small green chilli, chopped	*1*	*1*	*1*

1. Heat the ghee or oil in a heavy-bottomed saucepan. Add the onion, garlic and ginger and fry until golden brown.

2. Stir in the ground spices and the crushed tomatoes and cook until the oil appears on the surface of the mixture.

3.   Then add the spinach and the paneer pieces.

4.   Cover the saucepan and leave to simmer on medium-low heat for a further 5-7 minutes or until the paneer is soft and spongy. Add a little water if necessary. Mix in the green chilli.

Serving suggestions

Serve hot with any bread, rice, lentil and rayta.

 Cooking time 15 minutes.

SUKHÉ MASALÉ DAR PANEER

Dry Spicy Paneer

This delicious paneer dish is very popular in my family. It is tasty and nutritious. You will find this dish of medium hotness.

Serves 2	Metric	Imperial	American
Oil	60 ml	4 tbsp	4 tbsp
Cumin seeds	2.5 ml	$^1/_2$ tsp	$^1/_2$ tsp
Medium onion, finely chopped	1	1	1
Large garlic cloves, crushed	2	2	2
Fresh ginger, finely chopped	1 cm	$^1/_2$ in	$^1/_2$ in
Ground coriander (cilantro)	5 ml	1 tsp	1 tsp
Garam masala	5 ml	1 tsp	1 tsp
Ground red chilli	1.5 ml	$^1/_4$ tsp	$^1/_4$ tsp
Ground turmeric	1.5 ml	$^1/_4$ tsp	$^1/_4$ tsp
Salt, to taste			
Can tomatoes, mashed	230 g	8 oz	8 oz
Paneer (see page 16)	150 g	5 oz	5 oz
Small green chilli, finely chopped	1	1	1
Green coriander (cilantro) leaves, finely chopped	10 ml	2 tsp	2 tsp

1. Heat the oil in a heavy-bottomed saucepan over a medium heat. Add cumin seeds and cook until brown.

2. Add the onion, garlic and ginger and fry until golden brown.

3. Stir in the ground spices, tomatoes and paneer pieces. Cook until all the liquid has been absorbed and oil appears on the surface of the mixture.

4. Mix in the green coriander leaves and green chilli.

Serving suggestions

Serve hot with any type of bread, lentil, rice dish and onion cucumber and tomato rayta.

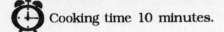 Cooking time 10 minutes.

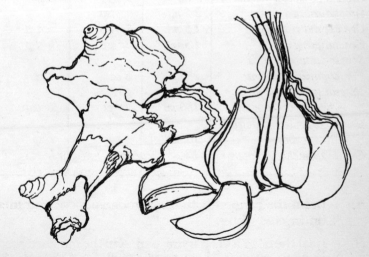

NAYÉ ALOO

Tangy New Potatoes

Potatoes cooked in tomato and yoghurt have a deliciously tangy taste. In this recipe I have used canned new potatoes, although I prefer the taste of fresh potatoes boiled in their jackets. Use the canned potatoes when you are really short of time.

Serves 2	Metric	Imperial	American
Can potatoes	410 g	14¹/₂ oz	14¹/₂ oz
Oil	60 ml	4 tbsp	4 tbsp
Mustard seeds	2.5 ml	¹/₂ tsp	¹/₂ tsp
Medium onion, finely chopped	1	1	1
Large garlic cloves, crushed	2	2	2
Fresh ginger, finely chopped	5 mm	¹/₄ in	¹/₄ in
Garam masala	5 ml	1 tsp	1 tsp
Ground coriander (cilantro)	5 ml	1 tsp	1 tsp
Ground roasted cumin	2.5 ml	¹/₂ tsp	¹/₂ tsp
Ground red chilli	1.5 ml	¹/₄ tsp	¹/₄ tsp
Ground turmeric	1.5 ml	¹/₄ tsp	¹/₄ tsp
Salt, to taste			
Can tomatoes, crushed	230 g	8 oz	8 oz
Natural (plain) low fat yoghurt	150 ml	¹/₄ pt	²/₃ cups
Green coriander (cilantro) leaves, chopped	10 ml	2 tsp	2 tsp
Small green chilli, chopped	1	1	1

1. Drain the canned potatoes through a sieve and rinse under cold water.

2. Heat the oil in a deep frying pan. Add the mustard seeds and when they start to crackle, fry the onion, garlic and ginger until they are light brown. Put in the whole small potatoes and fry for a further 5 minutes.

3. Stir in the ground spices and tomatoes and cook until all the liquid has been absorbed and the oil appears on the top of the mixture.

4. Mix in the yoghurt, coriander leaves and green chilli. Bring to the boil, reduce the heat and simmer for 2 minutes.

Serving suggestions

Serve hot with puri, plain rice, fried okra and urud ki sukhi dal.

 Cooking time 15 minutes.

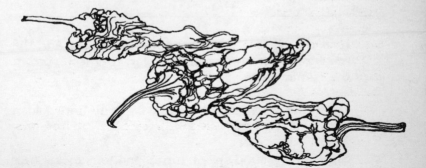

SHULGUM KI SABJI

Turnip Curry

This colourful dish is for all turnip fans. It is crunchy and you will find it to be of medium hotness.

Serves 2-3	Metric	Imperial	American
Oil	60 ml	4 tbsp	4 tbsp
Mustard seeds	2.5 ml	$^1/_2$ tsp	$^1/_2$ tsp
Cumin seeds	2.5 ml	$^1/_2$ tsp	$^1/_2$ tsp
Medium onion, finely chopped	1	1	1
Fresh ginger, finely chopped	1 cm	$^1/_2$ in	$^1/_2$ in
Garam masala	5 ml	1 tsp	1 tsp
Ground coriander (cilantro)	5 ml	1 tsp	1 tsp
Ground red chilli	1.5 ml	$^1/_4$ tsp	$^1/_4$ tsp
Ground turmeric	1.5 ml	$^1/_4$ tsp	$^1/_4$ tsp
Salt, to taste			
Turnip, peeled and cut into small pieces	250 g	9 oz	9 oz
Can tomatoes	400 g	15 oz	15 oz
Green coriander (cilantro) leaves, chopped	10 ml	2 tsp	2 tsp
Green chilli, chopped	1	1	1

1. Heat the oil in a heavy-bottomed saucepan. Add the mustard seeds and when they start to crackle, brown the cumin seeds.

2. Put in the onion and ginger and fry them until golden brown.

3. Stir in the ground spices, turnip and tomatoes. Cover the pan and cook over a medium to low heat for 15 minutes.

4.   Increase the heat and cook until all the liquid has been absorbed and oil appears on the top of the mixture.

5.   When the turnip is tender, mix in the coriander leaves and green chilli.

Serving suggestions

Serve hot with chapati, green lentil, rayta, aubergine and potato sabji.

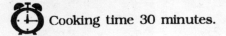 Cooking time 30 minutes.

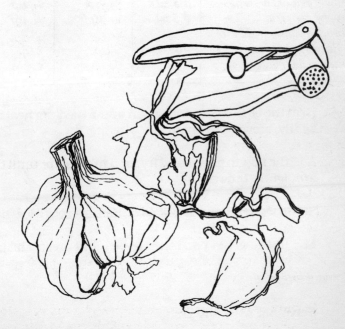

MASSALÉ DARALOO

Spicy Dry Potato

This dish provides a simple way to cook potatoes. You can boil the potatoes in their jackets in advance.

Serves 2	Metric	Imperial	American
Oil	45 ml	3 tbsp	3 tbsp
Small onion, finely chopped	1	1	1
Potatoes, boiled in jackets and cut into 1 cm (¹/₂ in) pieces	250 g	9 oz	9 oz
Ground coriander (cilantro)	5 ml	1 tsp	1 tsp
Garam masala	2.5 ml	¹/₂ tsp	¹/₂ tsp
Ground roasted cumin	2.5 ml	¹/₂ tsp	¹/₂ tsp
Ground red chilli	1.5 ml	¹/₄ tsp	¹/₄ tsp
Ground turmeric	1.5 ml	¹/₄ tsp	¹/₄ tsp
Green coriander (cilantro) leaves, chopped	10 ml	2 tsp	2 tsp
Green chilli, chopped	1	1	1

1. Heat the oil in a deep frying pan over a medium heat and lightly brown the onion.

2. Add the potato pieces and fry for 5 minutes or until they are lightly brown.

3. Stir in the spices and cook for 2 minutes over a low heat.

4. Mix in the green coriander leaves and green chilli.

Serving suggestions

Serve hot with any dish.

Cooking time 10 minutes.

Lentil Dishes

Dal means lentil, the different names being used in different countries are lentils, split peas, split pulses, split grain etc. It is the prime source of protein for vegetarian people

Dals are equally popular among vegetarians and non-vegetarian societies in India and they are cooked daily in every household. They are eaten with great relish with rice, chapati, paratha, vegetables, meat, fish and chicken. There are a wide variety of lentils all with different shapes, colours and sizes. The methods of cooking also differ in different parts of India.

In northern India 'urud' dal is cooked with garlic, ginger and asafoetida, in eastern India 'gram dal' (split yellow peas) is cooked with coconut and tamarind. In southern India 'arhar dal' is popular with a variety of vegetables and tamarind. In the western part of India 'moong dal' is prepared with lemon. Dal is delicious to eat and the fields where they grow are the farmers' joy.

Always clean dals before cooking. Pick out the stones and disintegrated grain because it is very unpleasant if they crack in one's teeth while eating. Try to soak the lentils before cooking. If you forget then add more water and cook a little longer. Indians prefer a fairly liquid consistency especially if the dal is to be eaten with a rice dish.

HARI DAL
Green Lentils

Without a pressure cooker, lentils take a long time to cook, therefore I tried this recipe with canned green lentils enabling you to prepare a delicious lentil dish within a short time. You will find this dish to be of medium hotness.

Serves 2-3	Metric	Imperial	American
Can green lentils	450 g	1 lb	1 lb
Ghee or oil	60 ml	4 tbsp	4 tbsp
Small onion, finely chopped	1	1	1
Fresh ginger, finely chopped	5 mm	$1/4$ in	$1/4$ in
Garam masala	2.5 ml	$1/2$ tsp	$1/2$ tsp
Ground red chilli	1.5 ml	$1/4$ tsp	$1/4$ tsp
Salt, to taste			
Can tomatoes, (mash with a fork)	230 g	8 oz	8 oz
Water	120 ml	4 fl oz	$1/2$ cup
Green coriander (cilantro) leaves, finely chopped	10 ml	2 tsp	2 tsp
Green chilli, finely chopped	1	1	1

1. Drain the tinned lentils through a sieve and rinse under the cold water tap.

2. Heat the ghee or oil in a heavy-bottomed saucepan over a medium heat. Add the onion and ginger and fry until golden brown.

3. Stir in the ground spices and tomatoes. Cook until all the liquid has been absorbed and the oil appears on the top of the mixture.

4. Add the lentils and the water and bring to the boil. Reduce the heat and cover the pan. Simmer the lentils for 2 minutes.

5. Mix in the coriander leaves and green chilli and serve.

Serving suggestions

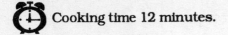

Serve hot with mushroom and corn, plain rice, chapati, chutney and sukha paneer.

 Cooking time 12 minutes.

DALÓ KA MISHRAN

Mixed Pulses

This nourishing dish is full of protein. I have used canned mixed pulses since fresh pulses take a very long time to cook. You will find this dish to be of medium hotness.

Serves 2	Metric	Imperial	American
Can mixed pulses	450 g	1 lb	1 lb
Oil	60 ml	4 tbsp	4 tbsp
Small onion, finely chopped	1	1	1
Large garlic cloves, crushed	2	2	2
Fresh ginger, finely chopped	1 cm	$^1/_2$ in	$^1/_2$ in
Desiccated (shredded) coconut	25 g	1 oz	$^1/_4$ cup
Garam masala	5 ml	1 tsp	1 tsp
Ground coriander (cilantro)	5 ml	1 tsp	1 tsp
Ground red chilli	1.5 ml	$^1/_4$ tsp	$^1/_4$ tsp
Ground turmeric	1.5 ml	$^1/_4$ tsp	$^1/_4$ tsp
Salt to taste			
Can tomatoes, crushed	230 g	8 oz	8 oz
Green coriander (cilantro) leaves, chopped	10 ml	2 tsp	2 tsp
Small green chilli, chopped	1	1	1
Water	120 ml	4 fl oz	$^1/_2$ cup

1. Drain the canned pulses through a sieve and wash under the cold water tap.

2. Heat the oil in a heavy-bottomed saucepan and fry the onion, garlic and ginger until almost golden brown.

3.   Add the coconut and fry lightly

4.   Stir in the spices and tomatoes. Cook until all the liquid has been absorbed and the oil appears on the top of the mixture. Add the mixed pulses and cook for 2 minutes.

5.   Pour in the water and bring to the boil. Reduce the heat to low and simmer for 2 minutes.

6.   Mix in the coriander leaves and green chilli.

Serving suggestions

Serve hot with rice, chapati, cauliflower and rayta.

Cooking time 15 minutes.

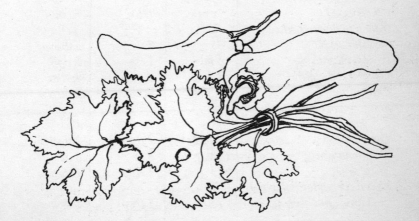

CHOLA DAL

Split Yellow Peas (East Indian Style)

Chola dal (gram dal or split yellow peas) is widely used in Indian cuisine, although the method of cooking varies between regions. I think that this dish with its unique sweet and sour taste, is absolutely delicious.

Serves 2	Metric	Imperial	American
For the dal			
Gram dal, cleaned and washed	125 g	4 ³/₄ oz	³/₄ cup
Bicarbonate of soda	2.5 ml	¹/₂ tsp	¹/₂ tsp
Turmeric	1.5 ml	¹/₄ tsp	¹/₄ tsp
Water	1 l	1 ³/₄ pts	4 ¹/₄ cups
Salt, to taste			
For the tarka			
Oil	60 ml	4 tbsp	4 tbsp
Mustard seeds	2.5 ml	¹/₂ tsp	¹/₂ tsp
Cumin seeds	2.5 ml	¹/₂ tsp	¹/₂ tsp
Small onion, finely chopped	1	1	1
Fresh ginger, finely chopped	1 cm	¹/₂ in	¹/₂ in
Coconut, desiccated (shredded)	45 g	3 tbsp	3 tbsp
Garam masala	5 ml	1 tsp	1 tsp
Ground red chilli	2.5 ml	¹/₂ tsp	¹/₂ tsp
Ground turmeric	1.5 ml	¹/₄ tsp	¹/₄ tsp
Small green chilli, finely chopped	1	1	1
Lemon juice	30 ml	2 tbsp	2 tbsp
Can tomatoes	230 g	8 oz	8 oz
Sugar	15 g	1 tbsp	1 tbsp
Green coriander (cilantro) leaves, finely chopped	15 ml	1 tbsp	1 tbsp

1.	Put the dal in a large saucepan with the water, turmeric and salt. If your saucepan is not large enough, keep boiled water ready to add to the lentils when required.

2.	Bring to the boil. Skim off any scum and simmer over a medium heat (place the lid on the saucepan leaving a little gap) until the dal is tender.

3.	While the dal is cooking, prepare the tarka. Heat the oil in a heavy-bottomed saucepan and add the mustard seeds. When they start to crackle, add the cumin seeds and brown them for 2 seconds.

4.	Put in the onion and ginger and fry lightly. Stir in the coconut and fry until golden brown.

5.	Add the ground spices, green chilli, lemon juice, tomatoes and the sugar. Cook until all the liquid has been absorbed and the oil appears on the surface of the mixture.

6.	Sprinkle in the green coriander leaves. Add the tarka to the cooked lentils and simmer for a further 2 minutes.

Serving suggestions

Serve hot with plain rice, fried okra, rayta sukha, masalé dar paneer.

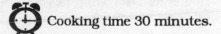 Cooking time 30 minutes.

SAMBAR

(South Indian Style)

This popular dish from the south of India is admired in all parts of the country. To make it as hot as the authentic south Indian dish, add double the quantity of red chilli. It is a bit complicated, but tastes superb. If you are short of time, cook the lentils and make the tarka described in the green lentil dish on page 92, and add 30 ml (2 tbsp) lemon juice. Lentils cooked in this way are called Arhar Dal.

Serves 2-3	Metric	Imperial	American
For the Sambar Masala			
Coconut, desiccated (shredded) or fresh, grated	50 g	2 oz	4 tbsp
Oil	10 ml	2 tsp	2 tsp
Whole coriander (cilantro)	15 ml	1 tbsp	1 tbsp
White lentils	10 ml	2 tsp	2 tsp
Split yellow peas	10 ml	2 tsp	2 tsp
Fenugreek seeds	5 ml	1 tsp	1 tsp
Whole small dried red chillies	4	4	4

1. Heat the oil in a flat frying pan over a medium to low heat and roast all the ingredients for 5 minutes or until light brown. Cool and grind to a fine paste.

	Metric	Imperial	American
For the Sambar			
Arhar dal (tuvar dal), washed and drained	100 g	3^1/$_2$ oz	3^1/$_2$ oz
Ground turmeric	1.5 ml	^{1}/$_4$ tsp	^{1}/$_4$ tsp
Bicarbonate of soda	2.5 ml	^{1}/$_2$ tsp	^{1}/$_2$ tsp

	Metric	**Imperial**	**American**
Salt, to taste			
Water	750 ml	2¹/₂ pts	5 cups
Aubergine (eggplant) or okra, quartered and cut into 5 mm (¹/₄ in) pieces	100 g	3¹/₂ oz	3¹/₂ oz
Tamarind, extract the pulp (see page 18)	50 g	2 oz	2 oz
For the Tarka			
Oil	60 ml	4 tbsp	¹/₄ cup
Asafoetida	large pinch	large pinch	large pinch
Mustard seeds	2.5 ml	¹/₂ tsp	¹/₂ tsp
Bay leaves	2	2	2
Small onion, thinly sliced	2	2	2
Garam masala	5 ml	1 tsp	1 tsp
Green chilli, chopped	1	1	1
Can tomatoes	230 g	8 oz	8 oz
Green coriander (cilantro) leaves, chopped	15 ml	1 tbsp	1 tbsp

1. Place the dal, salt, turmeric, bicarbonate of soda and the water into a large saucepan. Bring to the boil and skim off any scum. Reduce the heat to medium-low, close the lid and simmer for 25 minutes or until the dal is tender.

2. While the dal is cooking, cook the aubergine or okra in the tamarind pulp, bring to the boil and add the sambar masala.

3. Cook on a medium-low heat for 10 minutes or until the aubergine (or any other vegetable) is tender.

4. Mix in the cooked dal.

5. Heat the oil in a saucepan on medium heat for tarka (prepare the tarka while the dal is cooking). Add the asafoetida and the mustard seeds. When they start to crackle, put in the onion and curry leaves and fry them until light brown.

6. Stir in the garam masala, green chilli and the tomatoes and cook until all the liquid has been absorbed and the oil appears on the surface of the mixture.

7. Add the coriander leaves. Mix in the cooked dal. Bring to the boil, reduce the heat to low and simmer for 2 minutes.

Serving suggestion

Serve hot with plain rice, rayta and cauliflower-potato sabji.

Cooking time 30 minutes.

MOONG KI DHULI DAL ✓
White Split Moong Lentils

Moong dal is easy to digest, because of this it is cooked specially for young children, old people and the sick. Having said this, it is very tasty and most people usually cook it once a week. It is of medium hotness.

Serves 2	Metric	Imperial	American
For the dal			
Moong dal	100 g	4oz	$^1/_2$ cup
Ground turmeric	1.5 ml	$^1/_4$ tsp	$^1/_4$ tsp
Salt, to taste			
Water	1 l	$1^3/_4$ pts	$4^1/_4$ cups

	Metric	Imperial	American
For the Tarka			
Ghee or oil	60 ml	4 tbsp	1/4 cup
Cumin seeds	2.5 ml	1/2 tsp	1/2 tsp
Small onion, finely chopped	1	1	1
Garam masala	2.5 ml	1/2 tsp	1/2 tsp
Ground red chilli	1.5 ml	1/4 tsp	1/4 tsp
Ground roasted cumin	2.5 ml	1/2 tsp	1/2 tsp
Lemon juice	15 ml	1 tbsp	1 tbsp
Green coriander (cilantro) leaves, finely chopped	10 ml	2 tsp	2 tsp
Green chilli, chopped	1	1	1

1. Wash the lentils and place them in a large saucepan with the turmeric, salt and water over a medium heat. Bring to the boil, skim off any scum and simmer for 25 minutes. Make sure you put the lid on leaving a little gap, or the lentils will boil over.

2. While the dal is cooking, prepare the tarka. Heat the ghee or oil in a heavy-bottomed saucepan and brown the cumin seeds.

3. Add the onion and fry until golden brown. Stir in the ground spices, remove the pan from the heat and set it to one side.

4. Add the cooked dal, lemon juice, coriander leaves and green chilli and simmer over a medium-low heat for 2 minutes.

Serving suggestions

Serve hot with rice, bread, fried okra, cauliflower and aloo and palak paneer.

 Cooking time 30 minutes.

URUD KI SUKHI DAL
White Split Urud Lentils

Urud dal is not easy to digest therefore to compensate you will need to add asafoetida, ginger and garlic which aid digestion. This dish is medium hot.

Serves 2	Metric	Imperial	American
For the dal			
Lentils	150 g	5 oz	³/₄ cup
Ground turmeric	1.5 ml	¹/₄ tsp	¹/₄ tsp
Salt, to taste			
Water	450 ml	³/₄ pt	2 cups
For the Tarka			
Ghee or oil	60 ml	4 tbsp	4 tbsp
Asafoetida	large pinch	large pinch	large pinch
Large garlic cloves, crushed	2	2	2
Fresh ginger, chopped	1 cm	¹/₂ in	¹/₂ in
Medium onion, finely chopped	1	1	1
Garam masala	2.5 ml	¹/₂ tsp	¹/₂ tsp
Ground red chilli	1.5 ml	¹/₄ tsp	¹/₄ tsp
Ground turmeric	small pinch	small pinch	small pinch
Green coriander (cilantro) leaves, chopped	10 ml	2 tsp	2 tsp
Small green chilli, chopped	1	1	1
Lemon, cut into small pieces	¹/₂	¹/₂	¹/₂

1.   Wash the lentils and place them with the turmeric, salt and water into a large saucepan. Bring to the boil, skim off any scum and simmer on a low heat for 25 minutes or until the dal is tender.

2.   If any water is left, dry it off on a high heat, but do not stir or the dal will become mushy.

3.   While the dal is cooking, prepare the tarka. Heat the ghee or oil in a heavy-bottomed saucepan. Add the asafoetida, garlic, ginger and the onion and fry gently until they are golden brown.

4.   Mix in the garam masala, red chilli and turmeric. Remove the pan from the heat and set to one side. Stir in the cooked dal.

5.   Sprinkle in the green coriander leaves and green chilli. Squeeze over the fresh lemon according to your taste.

Serving suggestions

Serve hot with chapati or onion paratha, bitter gourd, stuffed aubergine, gajar-matar ki sabji, potato curry and rayta.

Cooking time 30 minutes.

Rice Dishes

India is one of the world's most famous rice producing countries. The world famous long grain Patna and Basmati rice are both produced there. Eastern and Southern India consume the most rice, but lavish biryanies and rice pulaos have originated from the northern part of India.

BHUNÉ CHAWAL
Fried Rice

Fried rice complements any dish.

Serves 2-3	Metric	Imperial	American
Rice (Patna or Basmati)	100 g	4 oz	$^1/_2$ cup
Cumin	5 ml	1 tsp	1 tsp
Small onion, sliced	1	1	1
Ghee or oil	60 ml	4 tbsp	4 tbsp
Bay leaves	1	1	1
Black cardamom, break open slightly	1	1	1
Black pepper	4	4	4
Cinnamon	2.5 cm	1 in	1 in
Cloves	4	4	4
Garam masala	5 ml	1 tsp	1 tsp
Salt, to taste			
Water	250 ml	8 fl oz	1 cup

1. Clean, wash and drain the rice.

2. Heat the ghee in a heavy-bottomed saucepan and brown the cumin seeds. Add the sliced onion and whole spices and fry until golden brown.

3. Put in the drained rice and dry off the water, this will take about 2 minutes.

4. Stir in the garam masala and salt.

5. Pour in the water. Cover the saucepan with a lid and bring to the boil.

6. Reduce the heat to minimum-low and simmer for 15 minutes or until cooked. Turn the heat off.

7. Open the lid and gently stir the rice with a fork. Place the lid back and serve after 5 minutes.

Serving suggestions

Serve hot with any dish.

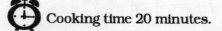 Cooking time 20 minutes.

MATAR MÉVÉ WALÉ CHAWAL

Peas Pulao with nuts

This rice is a nice weekend treat and suitable for entertaining friends.

Serves 2-3	Metric	Imperial	American
Rice (Basmati or Patna)	150 g	5 oz	2/3 cup
Ghee or oil	60 ml	4 tbsp	4 tbsp
Cumin	5 ml	1 tsp	1 tsp
Medium onion, sliced	1	1	1
Bay leaves	2	2	2
Black cardamom, break open slightly	1	1	1
Black pepper corns	4	4	4
Cloves	4	4	4
Cinnamon	2.5 cm	1 in	1 in
Garam masala	5 ml	1 tsp	1 tsp
Salt, to taste			
Frozen peas, thawed	125 g	4³/₄ oz	1 cup
Cashew nuts	25 g	1 oz	1/4 cup
Raisins	25 g	1 oz	2 tbsp
Water	250 ml	8 fl oz	1 cup

1. Clean, wash and drain the rice.

2. Heat the ghee in a heavy-bottomed saucepan and brown the cumin seeds. Add onion and whole spices and fry until golden brown

3. Put in the drained rice and dry off the water, this will take about 2 minutes.

4. Stir in the ground spices, nuts, raisins and peas. Pour in the water and cover with the lid.

5. Bring to the boil, reduce the heat and cook for 15 minutes or until the rice is tender. Gently stir with a fork. Turn the heat off. Cover the pan with the lid. For best result, serve after 5 minutes.

Serving suggestions

Serve hot with any dish.

 Cooking time 20 minutes.

BHUTÉ WALÉ CHAWAL

Sweetcorn Pulao

This is a very simple rice dish. In this recipe, I have used frozen sweetcorn, you can use canned sweetcorn if you prefer but make sure you drain the liquid and wash under the cold tap.

Serves 2-3	Metric	Imperial	American
Rice (Basmati or Patna),	100 g	4 oz	1/2 cup
Frozen sweetcorn (corn)			
thawed	100 g	4 oz	1 cup
Ghee or oil	60 ml	4 tbsp	4 tbsp
Cumin	2.5 ml	1/2 tsp	1/2 tsp
Small onion, thinly sliced	1	1	1
Bay leaves	2	2	2
Black cardamom, break			
open slightly	1	1	1
Black peppercorns	4	4	4
Cloves	4	4	4
Ground cinnamon	2.5 ml	1/2 tsp	1/2 tsp
Garam masala	2.5 ml	1/2 tsp	1/2 tsp
Salt, to taste			
Water	250 ml	8 fl oz	1 cups

1.   Clean, wash and drain the rice.

2.   Heat the oil in a heavy-bottomed saucepan over a medium heat. Add the cumin seeds and brown them.

3.   Add the onion, bay leaves and whole spices and fry until golden brown.

4.   Put in the drained rice and fry for 1 minute. Mix in the ground spices and sweetcorn.

5.   Pour in the water and cover the pan. Bring to the boil,

reduce the heat and cook for 15 minutes or until tender. Turn off the heat.

6.   Open the lid and gently stir the rice only once. Cover and leave for 5 minutes before serving.

Serving suggestions

Serve hot with any lentil, rayta, spicy peas or masaledar paneer.

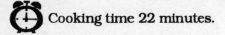 Cooking time 22 minutes.

MEEDHÉ KESAR WALÉ CHAWAL
Sweet Saffron Pulao

This dish was always cooked in our house on 'Basant Day'. On this day nearly every one in India wears yellow-coloured clothes. In Uttar Pradesh they celebrate the spring season and in Bengal worship the goddess 'Durga'. The traditional way of cooking this rice is a bit complicated, but I have simplified it for you.

Serves 2-3	Metric	Imperial	American
Rice (Basmati or Patna)	100 g	4 oz	$^1/_2$ cup
Water	250 ml	8 fl oz	1 cup
Green cardamom, use only the seeds	6	6	6
Ghee	45 ml	3 tbsp	3 tbsp
Sugar	100 g	4 oz	$^1/_2$ cup
Sultanas (golden raisins)	50 g	2 oz	$^1/_3$ cup
Cashew nuts	50 g	2 oz	$^1/_2$ cup
Saffron	2.5 ml	$^1/_2$ tsp	$^1/_2$ tsp
Yellow food colouring	2.5 ml	$^1/_2$ tsp	$^1/_2$ tsp

1. Wash and drain the rice. Place the rice, water, green cardamom seeds and ghee in a heavy-bottomed saucepan and bring to the boil over a medium heat.

2. Reduce the heat, cover the pan and cook for 10 minutes.

3. When the rice is nearly cooked, add the sugar, sultanas, cashew nuts, saffron and food colouring.

4. Stir with a fork, replace the lid and cook for a further 5 minutes or until the rice is cooked and all the liquid has been absorbed.

5.   Gently stir with a fork, cover and for best results serve after 5 minutes.

Serving suggestions

Serve hot after a meal.

 Cooking time 20 minutes.

TAHRI

(Uttar Pradesh Style)
Rice with Mixed Vegetables

Tahri is very popular in Uttar Pradesh. This rice dish is cooked with a mixture of your favourite vegetables. It is a very quick way of preparing a meal in one dish without much hustle and bustle.

Serves 2-3	Metric	Imperial	American
Rice (Patna or Basmati)	100 g	4 oz	$^1/_2$ cup
Ghee or oil	60 ml	4 tbsp	4 tbsp
Cumin seeds	5 ml	1 tsp	1 tsp
Medium onion, thinly sliced	1	1	1
Vegetables green (bell) pepper, aubergine (eggplant), potato, fresh tomato, cauliflower or any other, cut into 1 cm ($^1/_2$ in) pieces	250 g	9 oz	9 oz
Garam masala	5 ml	1 tsp	1 tsp
Ground roasted cumin	2.5 ml	$^1/_2$ tsp	$^1/_2$ tsp
Ground red chilli	1.5 ml	$^1/_4$ tsp	$^1/_4$ tsp
Ground turmeric	1.5 ml	$^1/_4$ tsp	$^1/_4$ tsp
Salt to taste			
Water	250 ml	8 fl oz	1 cup
Lemon juice	30 ml	2 tbsp	2 tbsp

1. Wash and drain the rice. Heat the ghee or oil in a heavy-bottomed saucepan over a medium heat. Add the cumin seeds and brown them, this will take 2 seconds.

2. Put in the onion and fry until golden brown.

3. Add the vegetables and rice and fry for a further 2 minutes.

4. Mix in the ground spices.

5. Pour in the water. Bring to the boil, reduce the heat and cover with the lid. Cook for 15 minutes or until tender.

6. Open the lid, tip the pan a little to see if there is any water. If there is water, increase the heat to dry it, but do not stir.

7. Add the lemon juice and stir gently with a fork. Replace the lid, leave for 5 minutes and serve.

Serving suggestions

Serve hot with pickle or chutney and yoghurt. Paneer tikka and baby aubergines go superbly with this dish.

Cooking time 30 minutes.

Nariyal-Sabji walé Chawal

Vegetable Pulao with Coconut

Rice cooked in tomato and coconut is really delicious and very popular in my house.

Serves 2	Metric	Imperial	American
Rice (Patna or Basmati)	100 g	4 oz	1/2 cup
Ghee or oil	60 ml	4 tbsp	4 tbsp
Cumin seeds	5 ml	1 tsp	1 tsp
Medium onion, sliced	1	1	1
Bay leaves	2	2	2
Black cardamom	1	1	1
Black peppercorns	4	4	4
Clove	4	4	4
Cinnamon	2.5 cm	1 in	1 in
Coconut, desiccated (shredded)	25 g	1 oz	1/4 cup
Garam masala	5 ml	1 tsp	1 tsp
Salt, to taste			
Frozen mixed vegetables, thawed	100 g	4 oz	1 cup
Can tomatoes	230 g	8 oz	8 oz
Water	250 ml	8 fl oz	1 cup

1. Clean, wash and drain the rice.

2. Heat the ghee in a heavy-bottomed saucepan on medium heat and brown the cumin seeds. Add the onion, bay leaves and whole spices and lightly brown.

3. Mix in the coconut and fry until it is also lightly brown.

4. Stir in the ground spices and tomatoes. Cook until all the liquid has been absorbed.

5. Put in the drained rice and dry off the water, this will take about 2 minutes. Mix in the thawed vegetables.

6. Pour in the water, cover with the lid and cook for 15 minutes on a low heat or until the rice is cooked.

7. Gently stir the pulao with a fork, cover and for best results serve after 5 minutes.

Serving suggestions

Serve hot with rayta, bitter gourd and puri.

Cooking time 25 minutes.

SADÉ CHAWAL

Plain Rice

In some parts of India, people always have a little rice with their meals. Plain rice, or as my children call it 'white rice' is prepared for daily consumption. It is very simple and easy to make.

Serves 2	Metric	Imperial	American
Rice (Patna or Basmati), cleaned, washed and drained	225 g	8 oz	1 cup
Water	450 ml	16 fl oz	2 cups
Ghee	15 ml	1 tbsp	1 tbsp
Salt	a pinch	a pinch	a pinch

1.   Place the rice, ghee, salt and water in a saucepan. Bring to the boil over a medium heat.

2.   Reduce the heat, cover the pan and cook for 15 minutes (if any water is left, dry it off on a high heat).

3.   Turn off the heat. Gently stir the rice with a fork. Put the lid back on. Leave for 5 minutes before serving.

Serving suggestions

Serve hot with any lentils, vegetables, chutney, pickle and rayta.

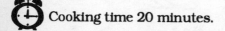 Cooking time 20 minutes.

Breads

Bread plays an important part in Indian cooking. Nan, paratha, bhutoora are the most popular breads of north India. South India's famous breads are Dosa and Idli, these are made with lentils and rice.

BHUTOORA

Bhutoora is one of the special and original breads from the Punjab. This is a quick and easy way of making bhutoora dough. Make the dough before you start cutting and chopping the vegetables for the rest of your meal.

Makes 8	Metric	Imperial	American
Self-raising (self-rising) flour, sifted	200 g	7 oz	1³/₄ cups
Margarine	15 g	¹/₂ oz	1 tbsp
Natural (plain) yoghurt	100 g	4 oz	¹/₂ cup
Salt	large pinch	large pinch	large pinch
Oil for frying			

To make the dough

1. Rub the margarine and salt into the flour.
    Mix in the yoghurt to make a soft, but not sticky dough. Add some milk if needed.
    Knead the dough for about 2 minutes or until the dough is springy and satiny.
    Cover and leave in a warm place for at least 30 minutes.

2. Divide the dough into about 8 equal portions and roll each portion into a ball.

3. Although the bread may be rolled out using a rolling pin, it is traditional to flatten the balls of dough between the palms of your hands. Put a little oil on each palm and pass the dough quickly from one hand to the other, flattening it until it is only 1mm thick.

4.   Heat the oil in a deep frying pan on high heat. Slip the bhutoora into the hot oil from the edge of the pan. Gently press the bhutoora with a slotted spoon all over and it will rise like a balloon. Turn the bhutoora over at the edge of the pan and fry the other side so that it is also light brown

5.   I always roll another bhutoora while the previous one is frying.

Serving suggestion

Serve with chickpea curry, rayta, sukha paneer, cauli-flower or baby aubergine. The bhutooras can be reheated under the grill.

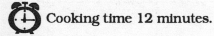 Cooking time 12 minutes.

CHAPATI

Chapati is eaten every day in most parts of India, because it is quite simple to make and easy to digest. I prefer to make chapaties with brown chapati flour, but if this is unavailable then you can make them by mixing together equal quantities of wholemeal and plain flour. Chapati is also known as roti or phulka.

Makes 6	Metric	Imperial	American
Chapati flour	*225 g*	*8 oz*	*2 cups*
Lukewarm water	*120 ml*	*4 fl oz*	*1/2 cup*
Butter or ghee to smear			

To make the dough

1. Put aside a handful of flour for rolling-out and place the remaining chapati flour in a bowl. Gradually pour in the water to make a soft, but not sticky, dough.

2. Knead for 1 minute or until the dough is springy and satiny. Cover and set aside for 10 minutes.

To make the chapati

1. Divide the dough into 6 equal portions. Take a portion of dough and roll it between the palm of your hands. Flatten, and dust in dry flour.

2. Roll the flattened dough out on a rolling board into a thin 2 mm round circle.

3. Heat a flat frying pan on medium heat. Place the chapati in the pan and cook for about 1 minute, turn over and lightly cook on the other side making sure that all the edges are cooked. Turn again and press the chapati gently with a clean cloth and it will rise like a balloon, this will take 30-45 seconds. I roll my next chapati while one is cooking.

4. Smear one face of the cooked chapati with 5 ml/1 tsp butter or ghee.

Serving suggestion

Serve hot with all sorts of curries.

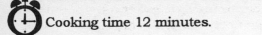 Cooking time 12 minutes.

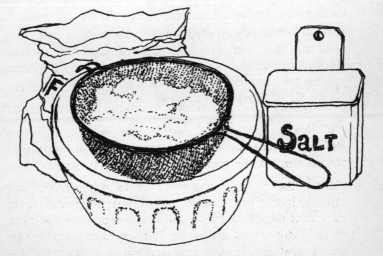

NAN

This recipe enables you to make nan bread without preparing the dough 2 hours in advance. Still your nans will be just perfect. Make the dough just before you start preparing the rest of your meal.

Makes 6	Metric	Imperial	American
Preparing the dough			
Self-raising (self-rising) flour	300 g	11 oz	2³/₄ cups
Bicarbonate of soda	2.5 ml	¹/₂ tsp	¹/₂ tsp
Margarine, diced	25 g	1 oz	2 tbsp
Natural (plain) yoghurt	30 ml	2 tbsp	2 tbsp
Milk	100 ml	3¹/₂ fl oz	6¹/₂ tbsp
Salt	small pinch	small pinch	small pinch

To make the dough

1. Rub the margarine, yoghurt, bicarbonate of soda and salt into the flour. Add the milk and knead the dough for about 2 minutes or until the dough is springy and satiny and add a little more milk if necessary. Cover and leave for at least 30 minutes.

2. Divide the dough into 6 equal portions. Take a piece of dough, flatten it and make a round or an oblong shape by patting it with your hand. It should be about 5 mm (¹/₄ in) thick. Grease the grill tray with oil. Depending upon the size of your grill tray, you may need to cook the nans in batches.

3. Place the nans on the tray and brush the top with water. I usually wet my hand under the tap and wet the top of the nan before placing it on the tray. Grill until golden brown. Turn them over and again smear the top with water. Cook the other side until golden brown.

4. Take the nan out and smear the top with butter or ghee. One tray of nans should take about 5 minutes to cook.

Serving suggestions

Serve hot with any curry.

Cooking time 10 minutes.

ONION PARATHA

Onion paratha is one of the simplest parathas to make; it is a popular item for children's packed lunch boxes, picnics and journeys. It is also served at breakfast with pickle or yoghurt.

Makes 5	Metric	Imperial	American
Brown chapati flour	225 g	8 oz	2 cups
Small onion, finely chopped	1	1	1
Small green chilli, finely chopped	1	1	1
Green coriander (cilantro) leaves, chopped	15 ml	1 tbsp	1 tbsp
Oil	15 ml	1 tbsp	1 tbsp
Garam masala	5 ml	1 tsp	1 tsp
Tymol seeds (ajwain)	2.5 ml	$^1/_2$ tsp	$^1/_2$ tsp
Ground red chilli	1.5 ml	$^1/_4$ tsp	$^1/_4$ tsp
Salt to taste			
Water, lukewarm	100 ml	$3^1/_2$ fl oz	$6^1/_2$ tbsp
Butter or ghee to smear			
Oil for frying			

To make the dough

1. Place all the above ingredients except, for a handful of flour into a large bowl and mix well. Gradually pour in the water and make a soft, but not sticky dough.

2. Knead for 2 minutes or until the dough is springy and satiny. Cover and leave for 10 minutes.

3. Heat a flat frying pan over a medium heat. While the frying pan is heating divide the dough into 5 equal portions.

4.   Take a portion of dough and roll it into a ball in the palm of your hands. Dust it with flour, flatten it and roll it into a small circle. Smear one half with 2.5 ml (¹/₂ tsp) ghee or butter and fold over the other half. Again smear half with ghee and fold to form a triangle. Cover with a little dry flour and roll out to 3 mm (¹/₈ in) thick retaining the triangle shape.

5.   Place the onion paratha in the hot frying pan and cook both sides dry like a chapati. Smear 7.5 ml (¹/₂ tsp) oil over, fry the first side until light brown. Make 6 or 7 small slits in the paratha. Pour another 7.5 ml (1¹/₂ tsp) oil over the other side and fry until light golden brown. I roll my next paratha while the first one is cooking.

Serving suggestion

Serve hot with pickle, butter, natural yoghurt, fried okra, and white split urud lentil.

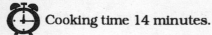 Cooking time 14 minutes.

Variation

METHI PARATHA
Fenugreek leaves paratha (bread)

Follow the recipe for onion paratha, but substitute 30 ml (2 tbsp) chopped methi leaves or 15 ml (1 tbsp) dry methi leaves instead of the onion. Roll to a triangular shape, like the onion paratha, or a square shape. For a square shape—roll a dough ball in a small circle, smear with butter or ghee and bring the edges over to make a rectangle. Smear the top again with butter of ghee and bring the edges over to make a square. Dust it with flour and thinly roll it into a square shape. Fry and serve as for onion paratha.

ALOO PARATHA
Potato Paratha

This is a popular bread which is cooked all over India. It is suitable for breakfast, lunch, picnics, and children's packed lunches.

Makes 4	Metric	Imperial	American
For the dough			
Chapati flour, brown	125 g	4 ¾ oz	1 cup
Oil	10 ml	2 tsp	2 tsp
Salt	pinch	pinch	pinch
Water, lukewarm	60 ml	4 tbsp	4 tbsp
For the filling			
Potatoes boiled in jackets, peeled and mashed	200 g	7 oz	1¾ cups
Green coriander (cilantro) leaves, chopped	15 ml	1 tbsp	1 tbsp
Lemon juice	10 ml	2 tsp	2 tsp
Garam masala	2.5 ml	½ tsp	½ tsp
Ground red chilli	1.5 ml	¼ tsp	¼ tsp
Tymol seed, ajwain	1.5 ml	¼ tsp	¼ tsp
Small onion, finely chopped	1	1	1
Small green chilli, finely chopped	1	1	1
Salt, to taste			
Oil for frying			

To make the dough

1. Place 100 g (4 oz/1 cup) flour into a bowl, keep the rest of the flour for rolling out. Rub in the oil and add the salt. Gradually pour in the water to make a soft, but not sticky dough.

2. Knead it for about 1 minute or until the dough is springy and satiny. Cover and leave for 5 minutes.

To make the filling

3. Place the ingredients for the filling into a bowl and mix thoroughly. Divide into 4 equal portions.

4. Heat a flat frying pan over a medium heat and while the frying pan is heating, divide the dough into four equal portions.

5. Take a portion of dough and roll it into a ball in the palm of your hand. Dust it with flour, flatten it and roll it into a small round shape.

6. Place one portion of filling on to the rolled portion of dough and bring the edges together to cover. Flatten the filled dough, dust with flour and roll it into a round shape, about 3 mm (^{1}/$_8$ in) thick.

7. Place the aloo paratha in the hot frying pan and cook both sides dry like a chapati. Pour 7.5 ml (1^1/$_2$ tsp) oil over it and fry the first side until light brown. Make 6 or 7 slits in the paratha. Pour over another 7.5 ml (1^1/$_2$ tsp) oil and fry the other side until light golden brown. I always roll my next paratha while the first one is cooking.

Serving suggestions

Serve it hot or cold (depending on where you are eating it), with plain yoghurt, pickle and butter.

 Cooking time 12 minutes.

MOOLI PARATHA

White Radish Paratha

Mooli paratha is a popular Punjabi dish. It is crunchy and has a distinct flavour. When salt is added to the radish, it will be necessary to drain or squeeze out the moisture.

Makes 5	Metric	Imperial	American
For the dough			
Chapati flour	250 g	9 oz	2$^{1}/_4$ cups
Oil	15 ml	1 tbsp	1 tbsp
Salt, to taste			
Lukewarm water	120 ml	4 fl oz	$^{1}/_2$ cup
For the filling			
Medium white radish, scraped and grated	1	1	1
Green coriander (cilantro) leaves, chopped	15 ml	1 tbsp	1 tbsp
Garam masala	5 ml	1 tsp	1 tsp
Ground red chilli	1.5 ml	$^{1}/_4$ tsp	$^{1}/_4$ tsp
Green chilli, chopped	1	1	1
Salt, to taste			

To make the dough

1. Keep aside a handful of flour for rolling out. Place the remaining chapati flour, oil and a small pinch of salt in a bowl and mix together thoroughly.

2. Gradually pour in the water to make a soft, but not sticky dough. Knead it for 2 minutes or until the dough is springy and satiny. Cover and leave for 10 minutes.

To make the filling

3.   Place the filling ingredients in a bowl, mix well and divide the filling into 5 equal portions.

4.   Heat a flat frying pan over a medium heat.

5   While the pan is heating, divide the dough into 5 equal portions. Take a portion of dough, and divide it again into two equal portions. Dust it with dry flour and roll in the palm of your hands two rounds, about 5 cm (2 in) in diameter.

6.   Sprinkle the flour on the rolling board and place one round of dough on it. Take a portion of filling, squeeze out all the water with your palm, place on one round of dough and cover it with a second round. Press the edges to seal, sprinkle some dry flour over it, roll out thinly to 3 mm ($^1/_8$ in) and place immediately in the hot flat frying pan.

7.   Cook both sides dry like a chapati.

8.   Smear 7.5 ml (1$^1/_2$ tsp) oil over the paratha and fry the first side until light golden brown. Make 6 or 7 small slits on the paratha. Smear another 7.5 ml (1$^1/_2$ tsp) oil into the pan and fry the other side light golden brown as well.

    I roll my next paratha while the first one is cooking.

Serving suggestions

    Serve it hot with natural (plain) yoghurt, pickle and butter with any meal.

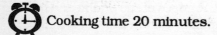 Cooking time 20 minutes.

PUDHA

Pudha is a lovely, crunchy mixture of gram flour (basin), onion and spices.

Makes 3	Metric	Imperial	American
Gram flour, sifted	75 g	3 oz	3/4 cup
Small onion, finely chopped	15 ml	1 tbsp	1 tbsp
Green coriander (cilantro) leaves, chopped	15 ml	1 tbsp	1 tbsp
Garam masala	2.5 ml	1/2 tsp	1/2 tsp
Ground red chilli	large pinch	large pinch	large pinch
Green chilli, chopped	1	1	1
Salt to taste			
Water, lukewarm	120 ml	4 fl oz	1/2 cup
Oil for frying			

1. Place the sifted gram flour, onion, spices and green chilli in a bowl and mix them together. Gradually pour in the water to make a smooth batter.

2. Heat a flat frying pan over a medium-low heat. Smear the pan with 10 ml (2 tsp) oil.

3. Place 30 ml (2 tbsp) batter in the frying pan and quickly and gently spread it with the help of a spoon until it forms a circle 1 mm thick. Cook it for 1-2 minutes, or until crispy and golden brown.

4. Turn it over with a flat or a slotted spoon. Pour 10 ml (2 tsp) oil all around the edges of the pudha and fry the second side until it is also golden brown as well.

Serving suggestions

Serve hot at breakfast with chutney, tea or lassi. It tastes quite nice wrapped in a slice of bread or placed on a slice of toast.

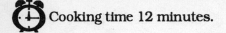 Cooking time 12 minutes.

PURI

Puri is probably the most popular bread throughout India. It is quick and easy to make and yet it is suitable for serving to guests. An average adult will consume about 4 puries.

Makes 8	Metric	Imperial	American
Brown chapati flour	200 g	7 oz	$1^3/4$ cups
Oil	15 ml	1 tbsp	1 tbsp
Salt	large pinch	large pinch	large pinch
Water, lukewarm	120 ml	4 fl oz	$^1/2$ cup

To make the dough

1. Place the flour in a bowl and rub in the oil and salt thoroughly. Gradually pour in the water to make a soft but not sticky dough. Knead for 2 minutes or until the dough is springy and satiny. Cover and leave for 10 minutes.

129

Frying the puri

2.   Fill three-quarters of your deep frying pan with oil. Heat the oil over a medium heat. While the oil is heating, divide the dough into 8 equal portions.

3.   Take a portion of dough and roll it into a ball in the palm of your hands. Flatten it, place a few drops of oil on the rolling board and roll it into a thin 1 mm round with the rolling pin.

4.   Slip a puri into the hot oil from the edge of the pan. Gently, but swiftly press the puri with a slotted spoon all over and it will rise like a balloon. Turn the puri over at the edge of the pan and fry the other side until it is also golden brown. I roll another puri while one is frying.

Serving suggestion

Serve hot with a meal. Puri goes superbly with any sort of vegetable, lentil or yoghurt dish.

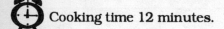 Cooking time 12 minutes.

Variation

TYMOL PURI
AJWAIN PURI

Ajwain adds a lovely taste to puries.
Follow the recipe for puri but add 5 ml (1 tsp) ajwain with the oil before you make the dough.

RAYTAS

Indians have done a lot of experiments with savoury yoghurt dishes. Yoghurt in different forms is used in Indian food because India is a hot country and yoghurt produces a cooling effect on the body. Yoghurt also reduces the effect of the hot spices which are used in the Indian food. The protein in yoghurt can be easily digested and absorbed by the human body. In India, yoghurt is usually made at home and if any butter is needed it is extracted from the yoghurt. In this process buttermilk is also formed which is used as a cold drink after a meal.

DHANIYA, PUDEENA WALA DAHI

Coriander and Mint Rayta

This is one of the most refreshing and delicious raytas and it can be prepared in minutes. Serve this rayta as an accompaniment to any Indian dish.

Serves 2	Metric	Imperial	American
Natural (plain) yoghurt,	150 g	5 oz	⅔ cup
Salt, to taste			
Green coriander (cilantro)			
leaves, finely chopped	10 ml	2 tsp	2 tsp
Fresh mint leaves, finely			
chopped,	10 ml	2 tsp	2 tsp
or dried mint	5 ml	1 tsp	1 tsp
Small green chilli, finely			
chopped	1	1	1
Ground roasted cumin	2.5 ml	½ tsp	½ tsp

1.   Whisk the yoghurt until smooth and leave to chill. Mix in the salt and add the chopped coriander, mint, green chilli, and ground roasted cumin just before serving.

2.   Mix thoroughly.

Serving suggestions

Serve chilled with a meal.

ALOO WALI DAHI

Potato Rayta

If you have any leftover boiled potatoes, then prepare potato rayta.

Serves 2	Metric	Imperial	American
Natural (plain) yoghurt	150 ml	5 oz	¾ cup
Potatoes, boiled in their jackets, peeled and diced	1	1	1
Onion, finely chopped	15 ml	1 tbsp	1 tbsp
Green coriander (cilantro) leaves, chopped	10 ml	2 tsp	2 tsp
Green chilli, chopped	1	1	1
Roasted cumin	2.5 ml	½ tsp	½ tsp
Salt, to taste			

1. Whisk the yoghurt until smooth and leave to chill. Mix in the salt and add the potato, onion and half the coriander leaves, roasted cumin and green chilli.

2. Mix together thoroughly.

3. Sprinkle over the remaining coriander leaves, roasted cumin and green chilli just before you serve.

Serving suggestions

Serve chilled with a meal.

TAMATAR, KHEERA AUR PAYAJ WALA RAYTA

Tomato, Cucumber and Onion Rayta

This is one of the most popular yoghurt dishes in India, and it is incredibly easy and quick to make. This rayta goes very well with most Indian dishes.

Serves 2	Metric	Imperial	American
For the rayta			
Natural (plain) yoghurt,	150 ml	5 oz	¾ cup
Small tomato, cut into 1 cm			
(¹/2 in) pieces	1	1	1
Small onion, finely chopped	1	1	1
Small cucumber, cut into			
1 cm (¹/2 in) pieces	¹/2	¹/2	¹/2
Salt, to taste			
For the garnish			
Ground roasted cumin	2.5 ml	¹/2 tsp	¹/2 tsp
Green coriander (cilantro)			
leaves, chopped	10 ml	2 tsp	2 tsp
Small green chilli, chopped	1	1	1

1. Whisk the yoghurt until smooth and leave to chill. Mix in the salt and half of the ground cumin.

2. A few minutes before you want to eat, add the tomatoes, onions and cucumber pieces.

3. Mix together thoroughly.

4. Sprinkle over the remaining garnish before serving.

Serving suggestions

Serve chilled with a meal.

Chutneys

The word 'chutney' is a Hindu word. Chutneys have been used as a form of preserving for hundreds of years and they make a refreshing and textually contrasting accompaniment for most curry dishes.

COCONUT CHUTNEY
South Indian Style

This cooling refreshing chutney is popular throughout India. The mixture of yoghurt, coconut, mint, coriander leaves and lentils produces a unique flavour. The chutney is hot and spicy, but the coconut has a cooling effect.

Fills 450 g/1 lb jam jar	Metric	Imperial	American
Natural (plain) yoghurt	150 g	5 oz	⅔ cup
Coconut desiccated (shredded) or fresh grated	75 g	3 oz	⅔ cup
Lemon juice	60 ml	4 tbsp	4 tbsp
Green coriander (cilantro) leaves	15 ml	1 tbsp	1 tbsp

	Metric	**Imperial**	**American**
Mint leaves	*15 ml*	*1 tbsp*	*1 tbsp*
or dried mint	*5 ml*	*1 tsp*	*1 tsp*
Gram dal, soaked in boiling			
water for a few minutes	*15 ml*	*1 tbsp*	*1 tbsp*
Ground roasted cumin	*5 ml*	*1 tsp*	*1 tsp*
Ground red chilli	*2.5 ml*	*$^1/_2$ tsp*	*$^1/_2$ tsp*
Fresh ginger, coarsely			
chopped	*1 cm*	*$^1/_2$ in*	*$^1/_2$ in*
Small green chilli	*1*	*1*	*1*
Salt, to taste			
For the tarka			
Oil	*15 ml*	*1 tbsp*	*1 tbsp*
Asafoetida	*large*	*large*	*large*
	pinch	*pinch*	*pinch*
Mustard seeds	*2.5 ml*	*$^1/_2$ tsp*	*$^1/_2$ tsp*
Urud lentils, soaked in			
boiling water for a few			
minutes	*5 ml*	*1 tsp*	*1 tsp*

1. Combine all the first 11 ingredients in a blender and blend to make a smooth paste. Place in a bowl.

2. Heat the oil in a small saucepan on medium heat. Add the asafoetida and the mustard seeds. When the mustard seeds start to crackle fry the lentils until light brown.

3. Pour this over the blended chutney paste and mix.

Serving suggestions

Serve with dosa, sambar and idli.

Cooking time 2 minutes.

TAMATAR KI CHUTNEY

Tomato Chutney

Fresh tomato chutney with vinegar is delicious and very easy and quick to make.

Fills 225 g/ ½ lb jam jar	Metric	Imperial	American
Oil	10 ml	2 tsp	2 tsp
Mustard seeds	2.5 ml	½ tsp	½ tsp
Fresh tomatoes, chopped into small pieces	250 g	9 oz	9 oz
Sugar	100 g	4 oz	½ cup
Vinegar	10 ml	2 tsp	2 tsp
Garam masala	2.5 ml	½ tsp	½ tsp
Red chilli	1.5 ml	¼ tsp	¼ tsp
Salt, to taste			

1. Heat the oil in a heavy-bottomed saucepan over a medium heat.

2. Add the mustard seeds and when they start to crackle, mix in all the other ingredients. Stir occasionally. The chutney should be ready in 6 minutes depending on the heat. Its consistency when ready, is a little runnier than jam.

3. When the chutney is cool, put it in a dry clean jam jar. If you keep the jar in the fridge and make sure that you take the chutney out with a clean and dry spoon it should keep for about a month.

Serving suggestions

Serve cold at meal times or at tea-time with savoury snacks.

 Cooking time 6 minutes.

DHANIYA CHUTNEY

Coriander Chutney

This chutney has an exquisite and unusual flavour. It is a hot recipe.

Serves 2	Metric	Imperial	American
Bunch of coriander (cilantro) leaves, chop the leaves and the tender stems coarsely	1	1	1
Medium onion, coarsely chopped	1	1	1
Small green chilli	1	1	1
Lemon juice	90 ml	6 tbsp	6 tbsp
Ground red chilli	2.5 ml	1/2 tsp	1/2 tsp
Salt, to taste			

1. Combine all the ingredients in a blender and blend to make a fine paste. The chutney will keep in the fridge for 2-3 days only.

Serving suggestion

Serve with any meal.

IMLI KI CHUTNEY

Tamarind Chutney

Tamarind chutney is not only delicious, but it is also an excellent source of iron and other minerals. It will keep for a long time in an air-tight container if a clean and dry spoon is used to take it out. The chutney is acidic, so while cooking use a wooden or stainless steel spoon. You will find that this chutney is quite hot.

Fills 450 g/1 lb jam jar	Metric	Imperial	American
Dry tamarind, soaked overnight *	100g	4 oz	4 oz
Jaggery or sugar	250 g	9 oz	2¼ cups
Garam masala	5 ml	1 tsp	1 tsp
Ground roasted cumin	5 ml	1 tsp	1 tsp
Ground red chilli	2.5 ml	½ tsp	½ tsp
Salt (or black salt) to taste			
Raisins	50 g	2 oz	⅓ cup
Dried dates, pitted and finely sliced (optional)	5	5	5

1. Extract the pulp from the soaked or boiled tamarind by sieving it thoroughly. Throw away the seeds and the sticks (the waste should not exceed 15 ml/1 tbsp).

2. Place the pulp over a high heat with the sugar and the ground spices. Bring to the boil, reduce the heat to medium-low and cook for 10 minutes.

3. Add the dates and the raisins and cook for a further 2 or 3 minutes.

4. Allow the chutney to cool completely before spooning into an empty jar.

Note

* If you are unable to soak your tamarind overnight, boil it in 300 ml (½ pt/1¼ cups) water for 15 minutes over a low heat.

Serving suggestions

Serve cold with your main meal or potato dumplings, onion bhaji etc. at tea-time.

 Cooking time 15 minutes.

SWEET SNACKS

Sweets have an important role in India and no function or festival is celebrated without them. Sweets are always distributed among relatives, friends and neighbours whenever a child is born; a marriage takes place; on birthdays; when someone has passed an examination; at a festival or any other special event. People in India will look for any opportunity to distribute sweets. It is a lovely idea which enhances any celebration and brings people closer to each other.

KAJU KI BARFI

Cashew Nut Barfi

Cashew nut barfi is one of the exquisite Indian barfies that people normally prepare or buy to celebrate special occasions.

Makes 9 pieces	Metric	Imperial	American
Cashew nuts	*50 g*	*2 oz*	*$1/2$ cup*
Milk	*60 ml*	*4 tbsp*	*4 tbsp*
Sugar	*50 g*	*2 oz*	*$1/4$ cup*
Ghee	*15 ml*	*1 tbsp*	*1 tbsp*
Essence, gulab or kevera			
water	*5 ml*	*1 tsp*	*1 tsp*

1. Grind the cashew nuts in a grinder until very fine. Place the ground cashew nuts, milk, sugar and ghee in a saucepan over a medium heat.

2. Stir continuously until all the liquid has been absorbed and the mixture is ready to set.

3. Add the essence and mix thoroughly.

4. Spread the mixture onto a greased plate in a square shape about 1 cm (½ in) thick.

5. Leave in a cold place for 45 minutes to set.

6. Using a pointed knife, cut cashew nut barfi mixture into 9 square pieces.

Serving suggestions

Serve as a dessert or at tea-time with any savoury snack.

 Cooking time 5 minutes.

CHENAMURGI BENGALI STYLE
Sweet Indian Cheese

Cheese is called 'paneer' in the Punjab and 'chena' in Bengal. The Punjabies use cheese to make exotic curries whereas in Bengal cheese is used to make soft, juicy and colourful sweet dishes. Both types of dishes are the specialities of their particular area and are rich in protein.

Makes 300 g/12 oz	Metric	Imperial	American
Chena (see paneer recipe - page 15)	150 g	5 oz	1¹/₄ cup
Sugar	50 g	2 oz	¹/₄ cup
Water	60 ml	4 tbsp	4 tbsp
Ground green cardamom	1.25 ml	¹/₄ tsp	¹/₄ tsp
Essence, kevera or gulab water	2.5 ml	¹/₂ tsp	¹/₂ tsp

1. Place the chena pieces, sugar and water in a saucepan over a medium heat.

2. Stir gently until the syrup is ready to set. To test this, place a drop of syrup in a cup of water, if it sets at the bottom then the syrup is ready.

3. Turn off the heat and add the ground cardamom and the essence.

4. Keep on stirring and coating the chena pieces with sugar, until they are cool and well coated.

Serving suggestions

Serve cold at tea-time with samosas, tamarind chutney, dalmod and barfi.

Cooking time 10 minutes.

KHEER
Rice Pudding

Kheer is popular all over India. Nuts, green cardamom, essence and saffron give an oriental flavour which is missing from canned rice pudding.

Serves 2-4	Metric	Imperial	American
Milk	250 ml	8 fl oz	1 cup
Can rice pudding	450 g	1 lb	1 lb
Sultanas (golden raisins)	25 g	1 oz	2 tbsp
Almonds, blanched and finely chopped	12	12	12
Pistachios, finely chopped	12	12	12
Ground green cardamom	2.5 ml	1/2 tsp	1/2 tsp
Sugar	15 g	1 tbsp	1 tbsp
Essence, gulab or kevera	5 ml	1 tsp	1 tsp

1.   Boil the milk in a large heavy-bottomed saucepan over a medium heat.

2.   Add the rice pudding, sultanas, half the chopped nuts, green cardamom and sugar.

3.   Bring to the boil. Reduce the heat and cook for a further 6-7 minutes.

4.   Remove from the heat. Add the essence and sprinkle over the rest of the chopped nuts before serving.

Serving suggestions

Serve hot or cold after a meal.

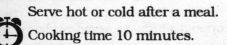 Cooking time 10 minutes.

NARYAL KI BARFI
Coconut Barfi

Coconut barfi is a lovely sweet dish or snack.

Makes 6	Metric	Imperial	American
Full cream milk powder			
(non-fat dry milk)	*50 g*	*2 oz*	*1/2 cup*
Double (heavy) fresh cream,			
whipped	*50 ml*	*2 fl oz*	*3 1/2 tbsp*
Ground green cardamom	*2.5 ml*	*1/2 tsp*	*1/2 tsp*
Coconut, desiccated			
(shredded)	*25 g*	*1 oz*	*1/4 cup*
Ghee	*10 ml*	*2 tsp*	*2 tsp*
Sugar	*25 g*	*1 oz*	*2 tbsp*
Water	*15 ml*	*1 tbsp*	*1 tbsp*
Food colouring, yellow	*2.5 ml*	*1/2 tsp*	*1/2 tsp*

Method

1. Place the full cream milk powder, cream and green cardamom in a bowl and mix thoroughly. Set the bowl on one side.

2. Place the coconut and ghee in a saucepan over a medium-low heat and fry for 3 minutes or until lightly brown. When cool, mix into the milk powder mixture.

3. Put the sugar, water and food colouring in the same saucepan over a medium heat and boil until it is ready to set. Test by dropping a little syrup into a cup of cold water. If the drop sets and stays at the bottom, it is ready. Remove from the heat and add to the milk powder mixture.

4. Mix it thoroughly until smooth and beginning to cool.

5. Spread the mixture on a greased plate and shape into a square about 1 cm (½ in) thick.

6. Leave it to set in a cool place for 3-4 hours. Cut into squares or triangles.

Serving suggestions

Serve cold after a meal or at tea.

🕐 Cooking time 5 minutes.

GULAB JAMUN

The gulab jamun is a delicious and popular sweet in India and it is served at almost all parties and on all special occasions.

Makes 8	Metric	Imperial	American
Full cream milk powder (non-fat dry powder)	50 g	2 oz	½ cup
Ghee, melted or oil	15 ml	1 tbsp	1 tbsp
Plain (all-purpose) white flour	15 ml	1 tbsp	1 tbsp
Milk, lukewarm	45 ml	3 tbsp	3 tbsp
Ghee and oil to fry (equal quantities)			
Sugar	100 g	4 oz	½ cup
Ground green cardamom	1.5 ml	¼ tsp	¼ tsp
Water	120 ml	4 fl oz	½ cup

1. Place the milk powder, ghee and flour in a bowl and mix thoroughly. Pour in the milk and make a soft dough adding more milk if needed. Cover and leave for 10 minutes.

2. Heat the ghee and oil mixture in a deep frying pan over a medium-low heat.

3. While the fat is heating, divide the dough into 8 equal portions and roll into small balls.

4. Add balls to the frying pan and gently fry until golden brown. Keep turning over. Do not fry too quickly or they will not be cooked inside. If the fat is too hot reduce the heat to low. Remove the dough balls with a slotted spoon and place them on a cooling tray. Repeat until all are fried.

5. While you are frying the gulab jamun, place the sugar, green cardamom and water in a saucepan to boil over a medium heat. Turn off as soon as the sugar has dissolved.

6. Add the fried gulab jamun to the syrup. Bring to the boil again, then reduce to a low heat and cook for a further 5 minutes.

Serving suggestions

Serve hot or cold after a meal or at tea-time with samosa or pakora.

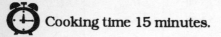 Cooking time 15 minutes.

BHUNI SEVIYA

Roasted Vermicelli

When I was 3 years old, my grandmothers taught me how to take a tiny piece of dough, twist it into a fine thread and leave it in the sun to dry. When the vermicelli was cooked, I used to climb onto my father's lap and pick the strands I had made out of his pudding!

Serves 2	Metric	Imperial	American
Milk	250 ml	8 fl oz	1 cup
Sugar	25 g	1 oz	2 tbsp
Ground green cardamom	5 ml	1 tsp	1 tsp
Roasted vermicelli, break the strands	25 g	1 oz	2 tbsp

1. Place the milk, sugar and green cardamom in a saucepan over a medium heat.

2. When the milk starts boiling, add broken strands of vermicelli and cook for 3 minutes.

Serving suggestion

Serve hot after a meal.

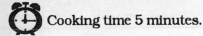 Cooking time 5 minutes.

SOHAN HALWA

The word 'Sohan' means pretty and 'Halwa' means sweet. It is also full of protein. You can make it any colour.

Makes 6	Metric	Imperial	American
Cornflour (cornstarch)	25 g	1 oz	¹/₄ cup
Sugar	50 g	2 oz	¹/₄ cup
Water	250 ml	8 fl oz	1 cup
Food colouring	2.5 ml	¹/₂ tsp	¹/₂ tsp
Ground green cardamom	2.5 ml	¹/₂ tsp	¹/₂ tsp
Ghee	45 ml	3 tbsp	3 tbsp
Almonds, blanched and cut into halves	12	12	12
Cashew nuts, cut into halves	12	12	12
Pistachios, cut into halves	12	12	12

1. Dissolve the cornflour, sugar and water in a heavy-bottomed saucepan and place over a medium heat. Stir until the mixture thickens and becomes transparent.

2. Add the food colouring, ground green cardamom, ghee, chopped almonds, cashew nuts and pistachios.

3. Continue stirring until the mixture comes away from the bottom of the pan and when you drop some from a spoon it falls in a lump.

4. Remove from the heat and spread the Sohan Halwa onto a greased plate, about 2.5 cm (1 in) thick and leave to set for 3-4 hours. Cut into 2.5 cm (1 in) squares.

Serving suggestions

Serve cold after meals or at tea time.

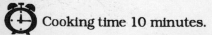 Cooking time 10 minutes.

SITAPHUL KA HALWA

Pumpkin Halwa

Pumpkin halwa is absolutely delicious with a unique and individual taste.

Serves 2	Metric	Imperial	American
Pumpkin, peeled and grated	750 g	1¹/₂ lb	1¹/₂ lb
Sugar	100 g	4 oz	¹/₂ cup
Water	250 ml	8 fl oz	1 cup
Ground green cardamom	2.5 ml	¹/₂ tsp	¹/₂ tsp
Almonds, blanched and chopped	25 g	1 oz	¹/₄ cup

1. Place the grated pumpkin, sugar and water in a heavy-bottomed saucepan over a medium-low heat. Half cover the pan with a lid.

2. Stir the mixture from time to time. Cook until all the liquid has been absorbed.

3. Mix in the ground green cardamom and chopped almonds.

Serving suggestions

Serve hot or cold after a meal.

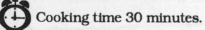 Cooking time 30 minutes.

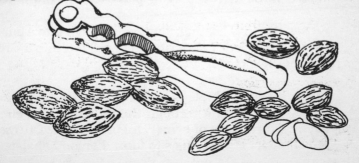

MEEDÉ SHAGARPARÉ

Sweet Shagarparé

This is a sweet snack which will keep in an airtight container for up to a fortnight.

Makes 400 g/14 oz	Metric	Imperial	American
For the dough			
Plain (all-purpose) white flour, sifted	200 g	7 oz	1³/₄ cups
Margarine	50 g	2 oz	¹/₄ cup
Water, lukewarm	90 ml	6 tbsp	6 tbsp
For the syrup			
Sugar	100 g	4 oz	¹/₂ cup
Ground green cardamom	2.5 ml	¹/₂ tsp	¹/₂ tsp
Water	60 ml	4 tbsp	4 tbsp
Ghee or oil for frying			

To make the dough

1. Sift the flour into a bowl. Add the margarine and rub it in thoroughly. Gradually pour in the water and knead for 2 minutes or until the dough is springy and satiny.

2. Cover the dough and leave for 10 minutes.

3. Place the oil in a deep frying pan over a medium heat.

4. While the oil is heating, shape the dough into a ball in the palm of your hands and then roll out into a 5 mm (¼ in) thick circle.

5. Take a pointed knife and make 1 cm (½ in) parallel lines, cutting right through the dough on the circle. Make a further set of 1 cm (½ in) parallel lines, to cross the first set of lines so as to form diamond shapes.

6. Put the diamond shapes carefully into the hot oil and fry them until light golden brown. Remove with a slotted spoon and set to one side.

7. While the shagarparé are frying, place the sugar, water and green cardamom in a heavy-bottomed saucepan over a low heat. Boil it until the syrup is ready to set (test by dropping a tiny amount of syrup into water, if it sets at the bottom the syrup is ready). Turn the heat off.

8. Put fried shagarparé into the syrup and keep turning them over until they are evenly coated with syrup. Leave to cool.

Serving suggestion

Serve cold at tea-time with pakora or after a meal as a dessert. They may also be served as a snack at a wedding or a party.

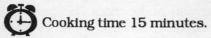 Cooking time 15 minutes.

Drinks

Most parts of India have long and very hot summers with intense heat waves. Soft drinks therefore play an enormous part in people's lives. Mostly people like to make and preserve different types of 'sherbert', 'dhandai', 'lasi', etc at home. The reason for this is that one can make them cheaper than buying them and they can be made according to one's individual taste.

DHANDAI

Chilled milk drink with nuts

Holi is the Hindu's most exciting festival. It takes place in April and celebrates the victory of God and destruction of demons. People visit each other's homes to play with gulal (dry coloured powder with a sparkling substance in it) and to throw coloured water at each other. They sing and dance on their way between houses. The host graciously offers them lots of sweets and snacks to eat and 'Dhandai' to drink.

Makes 6 glasses	Metric	Imperial	American
Almonds, blanched	5	5	5
Pistachio nuts	5	5	5
Milk	600 ml	1 pt	2^1/2 cups
Sugar	50 g	2 oz	^{1}/4 cup
Essence, kevera or gulab water	5 ml	1 tsp	1 tsp
Yellow food colouring (optional)	1.5 ml	^{1}/4 tsp	^{1}/4 tsp
Ground green cardamom	1.5 ml	^{1}/4 tsp	^{1}/4 tsp
Saffron	1.5 ml	^{1}/4 tsp	^{1}/4 tsp
Ice, to chill	6 cubes	6 cubes	6 cubes

1. Pour the milk into a large jug. Add the sugar and mix well until dissolved.

2. Stir in the rest of the ingredients including the ice. Place everything in a clean blender and blend for 1 minute.

Serving suggestions

Serve cold instead of tea during summer or with a meal.

EXOTIC MILK SHAKE

Chilled milk with fresh fruit juice and cream is a delightful and refreshing drink. It is an appetising way of taking protein and vitamins especially during summer when one may choose to eat less because of the heat.

	Metric	Imperial	American
Fruit (peach, apricot, plum, orange, pineapple or any other available fruit), washed and juice extracted	800 g	1¹/₂ lb	1¹/₂ lb
Milk	600 ml	1 pt	2¹/₂ cups
Sugar, to taste	45 ml	3 tbsp	3 tbsp
Kevera or gulab water or vanilla essence (extract)	5 ml	1 tsp	1 tsp
Ice cubes	12	12	12
To garnish			
Fresh double (heavy) cream, whipped until thick	150 ml	¹/₄ pt	²/₃ cup
Cherries	6-12	6-12	6-12

1. Blend the milk, sugar, ice and essence together. Pour in the fruit juice just before serving. Fill three-quarters of a glass with the milk shake, top with the cream and place a cherry in the middle.

Serving suggestions

Serve cold at breakfast, with a meal or any time you are thirsty.

MANGO SHAKE

Fresh mango shake is one of the most popular and delicious drinks in all parts of India especially during the summer season when mangoes are abundant. I love mangoes and when I was 2 years old I said, 'Mai apé naha lungi,' - 'I'll take my bath myself' because in the bathroom there was a big tub. This tub was filled daily with lovely big mangoes which were kept in ice cold water for the afternoon meal. I used to eat as many as I could and push the skin and the large seed (gudhali) into the drain but alas, I was caught one day by the sweeper because the drains became blocked. The first time I went back to India to visit my parents, they secretly arranged for eveything to be exactly the same and with a cheeky smile said 'Veena will take a bath by herself.' When I entered the bathroom I was surprised but thrilled to find the tub full of mangoes!

Makes 6-8 glasses	Metric	Imperial	American
Mangoes, peeled and chopped coarsely	2	2	2
Sugar, to taste	90 ml	6 tbsp	6 tbsp
Milk	1.2 l	2 pts	5 cups
Vanilla essence (extract)	5 ml	1 tsp	1 tsp
Ice			

1. Combine all the ingredients in a blender and blend until everything is mixed thoroughly and foam appears on the top.

Serving suggestion

Serve cold at breakfast and with meals.

LASSI

Yoghurt Drink

This refreshing cool drink is served during the summer in India at breakfast, instead of tea, and at lunch time, instead of water.

Serves 2	Metric	Imperial	American
Natural (plain) low fat yoghurt	300 g	10 oz	1 cup
Sugar add more if you like it sweet	25 g	1 oz	2 tbsp
Ice cubes, quantity depends upon the weather	4	4	4

1. Mix the sugar in the yoghurt until it dissolves. Place the mixture in a blender. Add the ice cubes and blend for 1 minute or until a lot of foam appears. Be careful not to blend for too long, otherwise you may get butter and whey from the yoghurt!.

Serving suggestions

Drink sweet lassi at breakfast sweetened with paratha, pudha, pakora or puri-aloo.

Variation

At other meal times Indians drink salty lassi to replace the salt lost through perspiration because of the heat. To make salty lassi: add salt, 1.5 ml (¼ tsp) ground roasted cumin 1.5 ml (¼ tsp) black pepper and 50 ml (2 fl oz/3½ tsp) water.

INDEX